STORM OVER THE STATES

STORM OVER THE STATES

by Terry Sanford

McGraw-Hill Book Company

NEW YORK · TORONTO · LONDON · SYDNEY

This book is dedicated
to the memory of
WILLIAM KERR SCOTT
Governor of North Carolina

Preface

During my term as Governor of North Carolina, from 1961 to 1965, I saw more clearly than ever before the many virtues in the systems of state government throughout the United States, varying, as they do, from state to state. It is difficult for anyone not directly involved to realize and appreciate the full range of activities, interests, and services of state government. I also observed a number of inconsistencies, flaws, and weaknesses. I became aware, too, that these deficiencies of state government had implications beyond the state itself, involving the future of federal and national government in America. For these reasons I have devoted a good deal of time and thought to looking for solutions to the many problems of improving state government. For the past two years I have had the help of a staff of three and the convenience of an office at Duke University provided by the Ford Foundation and Carnegie Corporation. The staff members, a lawyer, a political scientist, and a journalist, are Eli Evans, Thad Beyle, and David Ethridge. I have called this "A Study of American States."

I have not looked on this study as merely a research project, but rather have sought both to "do something" and to sound the trumpet for others who would labor to improve the states' effectiveness. Because I wanted a means of demonstrating that the states would act to strengthen themselves, and also because I was convinced that an idea of Dr. James B. Conant's [1] would serve the cause of improved quality in American education, we spent much of our first year putting together his suggestion for a Compact for Education. A result of this effort is the Education Commission of the States, with permanent offices in Denver. Some forty states are working together to make certain the states assume their full share of the responsibility for developing the opportunities for education required in America today. We also established, in our second year, a model for a kind of state self-starter, the Institute of the States, which is now operating the "Institute on State Programming for the Seventies," directed by Governor Jack M. Campbell (New Mexico, 1963–1967) on the campus and with the support of the University of North Carolina at Chapel Hill. I will describe more fully the aims and structure of the Commission and the Institute in the text of this book.

While working on these programs for action, we also took a practical look at state governments. We asked various panels to meet for several days at a time with us, and we drew upon their ideas and experiences. The panels consisted of political scientists and other academicians, former governors, newsmen and writers, and state planners. We also attended the meetings of other groups and associations of legislators and other officials and took careful note of their ideas. In addition to reading the appropriate literature, we attempted to gain additional insights by visits to most of the states and by a barrage of mailed inquiries to every state.

This book is not intended as either a text or an exhaustive treatise on state government, the federal system, or intergovernmental relationships. Numerous excellent studies and books are available, which I have drawn from and referred to rather than attempting to duplicate.[2] I have not intended that this book resemble a cookbook presenting all known recipes for state improvement. In the course of a number of years of observing, four years as Governor of North Carolina, and the two years of this study, I have gathered at least a thousand minor and major recommendations, all with some degree of usefulness. In this book I have tried to develop what appear to be the basic and urgent needs of the states, primarily those grouped around executive leadership. Later, perhaps, there may be time to pass on other suggestions gleaned from the helpfulness of those who believe state government must be renewed, as well as from those who have their doubts.

The purpose of this book is to give my impressions of state government. More specifically, my purpose is to express some thoughts on how the governments of the American states might be fashioned by the people to whom they belong so that they might serve both the immediate desires of the people and their enduring principles of government.

Duke University
Durham, North Carolina

1. James B. Conant, *Shaping Educational Policy*, (New York: McGraw-Hill Book Company, 1964).
2. I would recommend the following books as presenting a survey of these fields:

Charles R. Adrian, *State and Local Government*, (New York: McGraw-Hill Book Company, 1967); William Anderson, *The Nation and the States, Rivals or Partners?*, (Minneapolis: University of Minnesota Press, 1955); Daniel J. Elazar, *American Federalism: A View from the States*, (New York: Thomas Y. Crowell Company, 1966); W. Brooke Graves, *American Intergovernmental Relations*, (New York: Charles Scribner's Sons, 1964); Morton Grodzins, *The American System*, edited by Daniel J. Elazar, (Chicago: Rand McNally and Company, 1966); V. O. Key, Jr., *American State Politics: An Introduction*, (New York: Alfred A. Knopf, 1956); Duane Lockard, *The Politics of State and Local Government*, (New York: The Macmillan Company, 1963); Roscoe C. Martin, *The Cities and The Federal System*, (New York: Atherton Press, 1965); Coleman B. Ransone, Jr., *The Office of Governor in the United States*, (University, Ala.: U. of Alabama Press, 1956); William H. Riker,

Federalism, (Boston: Little, Brown and Company, 1964); and, York Willbern, *The Withering Away of the City*, (University, Ala.: U. of Alabama Press, 1964).

See also publications of the Advisory Commission on Intergovernmental Relations, The Committee on Economic Development, The Council of State Governments and The National Municipal League.

Acknowledgments

The polite thing to do would be to record the names of the hundreds of state officials and others who took the time to answer my correspondence, or to talk with my staff members or me, or to consult with discussion groups that met with us. It also would be almost impossible, and in some instances it might prove unfair to leave the suggestion that they had anything to do with the conclusions of this book.

I do acknowledge my deep appreciation to Paul Ylvisaker for his suggestion that this office be set up, and to Henry Heald and the Ford Foundation for supporting that suggestion. I also express my appreciation to John Gardner, Alan Pifer, and the Carnegie Corporation for adding financial support to enable me to study in greater depth the states' role in education and to explore the feasibility and wisdom of one device to strengthen that role, the compact for shaping educational policy which had been suggested by Dr. James B. Conant. In thanking the Ford Foundation and Carnegie Corporation of New York for granting funds that made the study possible, I take full responsibility for the statements made and views expressed in this book. I am grateful too for the hospitality of President Douglas Knight and Duke University.

I will always remember with warmth and gratitude my association with Eli Evans, Thad Beyle, and David Ethridge, a small staff, but a hard-working one, roaming across the problems we have attempted to define, as well as across the nation in quest of solutions and ideas for more effective government. Their contributions to me and my conclusions are beyond any normal measure. They join me in recording our thanks to Linda S. Hughes of Auburndale, Florida, whose husband attended Duke University Law School at exactly the right time to enable her to run our office and type this manuscript, both so capably and pleasantly. I am indebted also to Daniel J. Elazar of Temple University and J. O. Bailey of the University of North Carolina at Chapel Hill for reading this manuscript and making helpful suggestions.

Contents

I am free to confess that it had been my great ambition to be governor of Wisconsin, not just to be governor (for that seemed to me in itself but an empty honor), but to be in reality the chief executive of the state; to be a strong factor in securing legislation that should build into the life of the people a new order of things —laws that should be a recognition of human rights, that should make safe the vital principles of representative government. To aid in achieving such results was the realization of my highest ambition.

ROBERT M. LA FOLLETTE

STORM OVER THE STATES

CHAPTER I

Creative Tensions

The states are indecisive.
The states are antiquated.
The states are timid and ineffective.
The states are not willing to face their problems.
The states are not responsive.
The states are not interested in cities.
These half-dozen charges are true about all of the states some of the time and some of the states all of the time. On the other hand, at points in history, most of these charges have been applicable to both the national and local governments.

Admitting, for the sake of improvement, that there is validity to the charges, what can be done? If nothing much can be done, then indeed the states will soon be finished. And the federal system, the great compromise that brought together a wide and diverse land, will have collapsed.

Of course, something would evolve to replace the present system. It would surely be some form of unitary government. It would be a *national* government as distinguished from a *federal* government. On the face of it, as it now appears to be forming, it does not look bad. In fact, it looks more efficient. The regional offices of a completely national government would have dividing lines which make "sense." The lines of administrative authority could be drawn with more clarity. The bottlenecks, which some contend states are, would be broken. Policies and programs could be carried out with dispatch. No state could stubbornly slow down or stop a program that Congress had started.

We would have a clean-cut, efficient, neat governmental structure, capable of solving its problems, serving its people, and functioning without the confusion, muddle, and clutter of overlapping, competing levels of government that indeed were born out of compromise.

But this structure might not be what it seems. Although it might be shocking to admit, we should not try to have a neat government. Part of the genius of the American system of government is that it has been a bit untidy. More than we may realize, this has given us a flexibility, has permitted change, and has made innovation possible. If a proposal did not work in one place, it could be tried out in another. If an idea is turned down at one point, there is always another point where it might find acceptance. If something cannot be started or stopped in a state legislature, the advocates of doing something or stopping something can try city hall or their congressman. Neither the states nor Washington is the only port of entry for ideas, the single route to action, or the one blockade to mistakes.

The President rarely has his unrestrained way with the Congress. The troubles of John F. Kennedy, after his narrow victory in 1960, are much more typical than the legislative successes of Lyndon B. Johnson. It is far easier in Congress to beat something than to get it passed. Kennedy's problems were dramatized in a book by James MacGregor Burns, in which he pointed out that congressional deadlock was a common characteristic in American history, spotted as it has been with spurts of furious legislative activity.[1]

English politics rarely countenance disloyalty to the party line. The member of Parliament follows his prime minister or his leader of the loyal opposition. The English fail to appreciate the flexibility of our situation where a vote on any substantive matter is seldom without dissenters and line crossing from both sides of the aisle. Our broadly based parties have differences within their ranks, and the coalition shifts from vote to vote and subject to subject. Our freewheeling system, for all its apparent disorganization, is much more democratic and more creative than the English.

When some naturalists wanted forestry practices controlled but some insisted that control would destroy nature's balance in the wilderness, our untidy response was to have both. The U.S. Forest Service follows the first alternative, the U.S. Park Service the other, and the future has been better served.

Thus we can rejoice in a competitive, combative, contentious system that brawls its way to resolution and is provided with many openings for a fair hearing as well as ample safeguards against precipitate action. Some states permit liquor bottles on the table, some allow only mixed drinks, others insist that the bottle be under the table, and still others allow neither bottle nor glass. Not neat, but apparently it satisfies a lot more people than the uniform national approach once tried. When some states were enacting laws against closed-shop clauses in union contracts, others were either declining to do so or repealing such laws already on the books. There are strong arguments being made that this contract provision should be dealt with by one national law; there are also arguments being made against a single approach. Ours is a government with alternatives.

If the nation had a single divorce law, it would be much more restrictive than that of the most lenient state and more lenient that that of the most puritanical state. Who is wise enough to formulate for one and all the proper grounds for divorce in a nation as large and varied as this one? Twenty-three states this year considered changes in their abortion laws. That changes in a subject so delicate can even be discussed without a nationwide controversy over a federal law is a tribute to our diverse structure and a credit to the system. The very fact that in the enactment of such legislation some states may seem too lax to others is of value to society. The states are the outriders who test the limitations and restrictiveness of our accepted doctrines.

Capital punishment is another debated subject in which the cause of justice is well served by the options the states offer. If some contend that doing away with the death penalty will result in more murders, this opinion doesn't lead to an endless argument. Some state can try it. Michael V. DiSalle, a former governor of Ohio, makes the point that

. . . In the capital punishment states, a law enforcement officer's chance of being shot down in the performance of his duty is 1.3 per 100,000. In the abolitionist states, the rate is 1.2.[2]

At the present time, thirteen states have abolished the death penalty altogether. Some states have not abolished it by statute, but have done so in practice. Vermont, which has executed two men in twenty-eight years, abolished capital punishment except for repeaters and killers of policemen and prison guards. New York passed a limited bill, retaining it only for killers of policemen and prison guards. Tennessee developed its own technique. When the abolition of capital punishment failed in the Tennessee senate by one vote after overwhelmingly passing in the house, the governor commuted the sentences of everyone on death row.

The states test whether the opinions by which we live our lives and run our governments are myths or facts. This is federalism at its best—always probing, always testing, always seeking a better way. The states allow experimentation, change, and local leadership, especially in controversial subjects involving deep societal values in which feelings run high and attitudes vary all across the nation.

Neat conformity in government is found only in dictatorships. This price is too great. The fact that we have somehow understood this all along, that we have permitted and indeed encouraged a certain amount of flexibility and local adjustment has given added vitality to our development, and has brought many benefits over the past two hundred years.

The tension in our system stimulates competition, and the colliding loyalties encourage improvement. New ideas can surface close to home where local leadership can put them into practice with the confidence of the people. To smooth out this creative tension, then, is to waste resources. In every section of the country there are talented people who are devoted to their states and care about their cities. They are not apathetic, not selfishly protective, and they want to do what must be done.

No one locus of government has a monopoly on brains and creativity. Men with these traits follow leadership whenever leaders want to do the job. Mayor John Lindsay in New York City has assembled a first-rate group of men to pick up the reins of the toughest city anywhere. When Richard Hughes began to lead New Jersey and make its people conscious that they lived in a state, good men were attracted to his call. And in the national government, John Gardner took over a depressed and confused department and made of it the most creative place to work in Washington.

The challenge to the leadership on every level is to harness the bureaucracy to its goals. The governors and mayors share the goals of Washington's top leadership. They want to do all they can to improve education, help the poor, and find better jobs and opportunities for their people. Dismissing their suggestions, excluding their views, or disregarding their potential service undercuts the achievement of all the goals.

It is often the fashion to refer to state lines as obsolete, and therefore to treat state officials as provincial leaders of outmoded territories. But would neat and "sensible" state boundaries add anything useful to our system? Long before the New Deal, even in the nineteenth century, some political scientists were advocating regional governments to replace the illogical lines of the states. Admittedly the lines were not originally drawn with an awareness of developments to come in communications, transportation, and living patterns. But is the solution today to sit down together the best brains and computers for the purpose of redrawing them with calculated accuracy? Who has that wisdom and vision, even in tandem with computers?

Nobody can really believe that state lines will be redrawn. The Constitution stands in the way of that. Instead, new lines will come, if they do, as the invention of the technocrats after the atrophy and neglect of the present states. Then in disregard of the states and the old lines, the new administrative units of the national government could be shaped with some purpose in mind. The New York harbor would be neatly wrapped into one subdivision by some of New Jersey, Connecticut and New York State. Newark and Atlantic City would not be together; neither, for that matter, would Los Angeles and San Francisco. Each subdivision would be designed to carry out the national objectives.

No such fantasy will be started deliberately on a draftsman's board. But it might develop if the states and the cities, giving up self-reliance, lean too much upon national aid, complaining only that they must go to too many different regional headquarters to get what is coming to them and to find out what to do. If this fantasy did come true, it would probably start with the consolidation of all regional offices, according to logical lines, but as compromised out by the various agencies that already had field offices. For a while state boundaries would be generally followed in the groupings. Later it would make more sense, be more workable, to draw the lines according to terrain and population groupings.

The whole thing would turn out to be easier to teach in school. The lines dividing the country neatly into sixteen national administrative subdivisions or units (NATS) could be flashed on the wall-high television screen. Hawaii might cause some difficulty, but it could be tucked in a corner with an arrow indicating that it belonged to the Los Angeles NAT.

It would all seem so orderly and efficient. The governors and state legislatures would not have anything substantial to do. Many critical political scientists would write that it was good that congressmen still had to come from districts drawn within the old state lines. This, they would contend, had almost eliminated logrolling. The U.S. senators would be almost irrelevant, not that the administrative personnel would not pay attention to them. They would have to; they would still vote the appropriations. But since they came from states, they would not have much meaning as far as the administrators of the NATS were concerned. Since the unit boundaries would have to be drawn with population as well as distances in mind, it would have turned out that four of the NATS had only one senator, one had nine, and the New York NAT didn't have any. But this kind of drift could only follow an abandonment of self-reliance by the states and cities.

The ultimate aim of our political structure is not orderliness and efficiency, and it is not simply to break bottlenecks or avoid blockage by state action. The chief need of the federal system is not compactness and straight lines of authority. Instead, the citizens of the United States need diversified political strengths. Diversity, such as we have in our country, necessitates a federal system. Diverse political strength develops varied answers to assorted problems. It establishes the tensions for improvement. The power centers of the states protect our liberty from the possible tyranny of the national government, just as the power of the national government protects each citizen from the tyranny of the states.

The states are not merely subdivisions for administrative purposes. They may frequently act in that capacity, but they are more. They are, fundamentally, political units within a federal system, wherein both the parts and the whole rest on constitutional bases. No administrative subdivision could attain such a position.

Can we afford to let our present governmental relationships change substantially? We are moving into the era of joint responsibilities, the marble cake and the matrix, the partnership for seeking and solving problems, and the shared taxes. But can we allow one part of our federalism to become feeble, to lose position as a political force? The Articles of Confederation provided no power for the Congress, no way for it to withstand the political power of the individual state, no way for it to act for all the states combined into one nation. Consequently, the new nation was falling apart. The adoption of the U.S. Constitution eliminated that weakness. It created the power and authority needed for the states to act in unison. Now the question is, do we go to the other extreme?

The question can be posed very simply. Do we want a single national government, or a federal government which combines a national government with governments of the several states? The answer depends on our willingness to look for the faults and find the cures for the illnesses of state government. It is not possible to detail the disabilities of each state; some have one, and some have others, and some have too many to count. There is medicine to cure the illness and to put the states back on their feet. There remains the difficulty, however, of whether the people, the voters, want to take it.

1. James MacGregor Burns, *The Deadlock of Democracy*, (Englewood Cliffs, New Jersey: Prentice-Hall, Inc., 1963).
2. Michael V. DiSalle, *The Power of Life or Death*, (New York: Random House, 1965), p. 9.

CHAPTER II

People Are Government

"Government . . . is but a necessary evil," contended Thomas Paine in the emerging days of this nation. He was writing for and to those who, not quite knowing how, were pursuing a new kind of life in which they ordered their own affairs far away from the stifling hand of monarchy. The necessity admitted, Paine argued that the evil of government must be softened by placing the reins of decision in the hands of the people. In his own forceful language he expressed the colonists' uneasy and hesitant hopes: "Let the crown . . . be . . . scattered among the people whose right it is."

"In America," he said, "the law is king. For as in absolute governments the king is law, so in free countries the law ought to be king."[1]

Later in the same year, Thomas Jefferson, chairman of a committee of the Continental Congress, formalized the theme of Paine. He phrased in memorable words man's yearnings of many centuries: ". . . all men are created equal . . . with certain unalienable rights . . . that to secure these rights, governments are instituted among men, deriving their just powers from the consent of the governed. . . ."

The dream of self-government, however, was not the initial force drawing the Old-World citizen to the adventure and hazard of a new world. Probably the strongest force was the quest for a new kind of liberty, an individual liberty protected by an ocean of separation from the aristocracies, class systems, and "divine rights" of hereditary rulers. Most historians appear to agree that complete independence from the mother country, with attending self-government, was not dominant in the minds of the colonists for at least the first hundred years after Jamestown. Freedom was. But freedom to do what? Or from what? From oppression, from arbitrariness of the crown, of course, but the road to individual liberties had long been traveled in England. The colonists' hope was for a more exuberant kind of freedom—freedom, in all its implications, to seek opportunity.

The melancholy songs of the eighteenth-century poets reflected the gloom from which the colonists sought escape. Gray's plowman "homeward plods his weary way," passing his departed neighbors of the graveyard whose chances in life had been frozen by "chill Penury" and for whom "knowledge to their eyes her ample page, rich with the spoils of time did ne'er unroll." The common man's lot in life was to plod, his place in life was weary. But the beckoning new world, where "a man's a man for a' that," promised much more. On this new continent a man's destiny would not be fenced in by birth and rank. The landed nobleman wouldn't risk it. It would belong to those who preferred its risks and dangers to a life of secure but hopeless toil.

From the nebulous clouds of aspiration developed the thunderstorm of independence and revolution, the accepted price of individual opportunity. Self-government, it became apparent, was necessary to protect freedom, and freedom was the means of constant opportunity. After the revolution that created this nation, a turning point in the history of governments, the American dreamed of a land where a man could unchain his own society. His opportunities to build and achieve would be limited only by what he was able to do and willing to do. To be certain of this, government had to be his tool. Government would serve him, not he the government.

The major use of government, throughout American history, has been to expand and develop opportunity, while protecting liberty and freedom of action. The governmental performance, true, has been spotty. Often the opportunity of some has been unduly protected at the expense of the freedom of others. Often also one man's unrestrained liberty has meant the restraint of another's opportunity.

To preserve this delicate balance is the function of a self-government. It must protect each man's liberties. Yet it must keep open every man's opportunity. There has always been a hovering conflict, and the task of government has been to pull the thread with such dexterity that neither liberty nor opportunity became unstitched.

The opportunity to own slaves denied totally the liberty of those enslaved. When cheap wages or child labor were ingredients of manufacture, the liberty to make money largely negated the opportunity of others to make a good life. The liberty to exploit the minerals, the forests, and the rivers diminished the future opportunity of all the people of the nation.

From the very beginning, despite the quicksands of greed, despite the currents and eddies from the traditional European distrust of the voice of the people, the destiny of America has been to perfect the republican form of government which could be the bulwark of both freedoms—liberty and opportunity. Not always defined clearly, frequently distorted, never agreed upon unanimously, it is manifest that these have been the two guiding stars of American government.

So today the debate should not be defined in terms of state government versus national government, strength in combat with counter strength. Our question is not one of governments standing off each other, pitting force against force, jockeying for position, to shape the relative powers of state and national government. The citizens constitute both, and

ultimately the citizens must control both. The question is
not whether national government will triumph, or state government will triumph; but whether the citizen will triumph
in protecting his liberties while broadening his opportunities.
The result will be determined by the citizen and how he
shapes his historic and revolutionary federal system of governments within a government.

Today the plowman no longer plods. No longer is his relationship with his government obscure, and no longer are his
needs from government simple. Certainly he no longer moves
slowly enough to be observed from any country churchyard.
He speeds by in a car. New or used, it is in all likelihood
financed under terms whose interest rates, at least, are controlled by state statute. In his complex world he needs not
only protection from the usurer, but from other motorists and
from unsafe manufacturing standards, and he demands that
his government, on all levels, preserve him. If he travels by
bus or plane or train instead of in his own car, only his government can regulate, and even sustain, the methods of mass
transportation he requires. If he has a bank deposit left after
his car payments, his sad experience has led him to call on
his government both to superintend the banker and insure
the savings.

At his place of work his government has established a
minimum wage and protects his right to bargain for more.
It also prevents him from taking his child out of school to
work in a factory or field. If he reports to work and finds
a dismissal slip, he draws family support from his government
until he can find another job, which his government will help
him find, or will train him for another. When he grows too
old to work, he draws from an insurance fund his government has required him to help accumulate. If he gets sick
enough, he goes to a hospital built, in most cases, with his
government's funds, and government may pay his medical

expenses. Most certainly he will be treated by a doctor who received his training at facilities subsidized by his government. If he dies, he has already counted on his government to take care of his dependent children as well as his widowed and invalid mother.

His government keeps germs out of his milk, and bugs out of his corn flakes, puts chlorines and maybe fluorine in his drinking water, quenches the flame if his house catches on fire, gets electricity to his television set, or licenses some company to do so; it picks up his garbage, and kills some of his flies. It protects him from foreign invaders and local intruders. It keeps him from shooting too many ducks or rabbits. It educates his children and builds places for them to play and swim and look at zebras. It shows him how to plant beans and underwrites the price of his wheat. It builds roads for his automobiles, channels for his boats, airports for his planes. It locks up those who break his laws.

Government serves and responds to the citizen in all these ways and many more. He does not even breathe without governmental concern—and efforts to cleanse the air. Certainly he inhales tobacco smoke only after a printed warning from his government. In some of these ways he is served by his national government, in some by his state government, in others by a conglomeration he calls local government, but in most by the combined efforts of all three.

All of these services he has insisted upon, using his government to protect and improve his position, his chance, his opportunity. If he received the services from his local government he believed necessary for his advantage, he let it go at that. If not, he demanded that state government assist or assume the burden. If he could not crank this machine, he started pushing and pulling at his national government.

Senator Edmund Muskie tells of a road fork in Maine, where a tourist found signs pointing each way, both of which said "Portland." He beckoned to a farmer leaning on a hoe. "Does it make any difference which road I take to Portland?" he asked.

Came the terse reply, "Not to me it don't."

Much of the debate over which level of government should be given the authority over a particular program has been irrelevant to most Americans. They really have not much cared "which road we take to Portland." What has mattered, and still matters, is attacking the problem and getting the job done.

Along the Mississippi river front in the heart of downtown St. Louis, forty city blocks were cleared away for the Jefferson National Expansion Memorial. Its most famous landmark now is the towering gateway arch, symbolizing St. Louis' heroic role as the "Gateway to the West." On the walls of the historic old courthouse where Dred Scott once sued for his freedom a plaque says, "Administered by the National Park Service, U.S. Department of Interior." This is not an isolated triumph of nature like Yellowstone or the Grand Canyon; nor a virgin forest set aside for the protection of wild life and outdoor recreation. It is mostly the work of the national and city governments in the center of a busy and at one time decaying American city. Its purpose is to celebrate the pageant of the American pioneer and his conquest of the wilderness, and its incidental benefit is the revitalization of a crumbling downtown.

Man has not been wedded to the system of state sovereignty at the expense of his opportunities, as the movement of many state activities to the national government testifies. But this fact doesn't argue the validity or the virtue of centralized government. It argues, rather, that the citizen sees his various governments as his agents, and he is determined to use them for the purposes he feels beneficial to him. Nor does he intend to allow a strongly centralized system of government to provide new opportunities at the expense of his old freedoms. His growing concern about the increasing size of the national government testifies to this.

His quest, after all, continues to be for liberty and opportunity. The relative authority of governments, their shares of the burdens and the initiatives, and intergovernmental relations generally, must be shaped by the people on the basis of how these historic twin goals may best be reached.

If one way fails to work, the people will inevitably try another. And if the new way begins to appear dangerous, the people will draw back to a safer ledge.

At the 1965 White House Conference on Education, one panel discussed the pyramiding needs for more money in education. A comprehensive background paper was prepared on tax structures, wherein the financial resources of the national government were compared with those of the other levels of government. At one point in the debate, a distinguished elderly gentleman stood up in the audience and said, "What is all this talk about federal money and state money? It's not federal money. It's my money. I write the check to Internal Revenue. It goes into the kitty to help America. There ought to be no such thing as purse-string power. It all comes out of my wallet."

People are government, whether it is called state or national. The question for the future is how might our federal system of states within a state, a remarkable instrument of self-government, best be operated by the people to achieve their opportunities while preserving the liberties from whence their future opportunities will spring?

Is the federal government too centralized? The answer lies in how it serves the citizen. Is state government too weak and ineffective? The answer lies in how it serves the citizen.

Is the central government too powerful? Do we need better balance in intergovernmental divisions? Should state governments be called on for more extensive activity? The answers lie in how they serve the citizen.

If government is to serve the citizen, how does he go about perfecting the servant? The answer lies in what the citizen wants to do as he understands what can be done.

1. "Common Sense," in Philip S. Foner, (ed.), *The Complete Writings of Thomas Paine,* (New York: The Citadel Press, 1945), pp. 4, 29.

CHAPTER III

The Weakening of the States

When the United States Constitution was being written, replacing the Articles of Confederation, most participants believed the states should be subordinated to the national government. Some favored drastic subordination. James Madison of Virginia felt it imperative that the new Congress have the right to negative acts by the state legislatures. Charles Pinckney of South Carolina would have had all state laws approved by Congress before they could become effective. Alexander Hamilton, after having abandoned his earlier suggestion that states be abolished, was in favor of having state governors appointed by the federal government.

Left out of the new Constitution was the provision of the Articles of Confederation that *"Each State retains its sovereignty, freedom and independence, and every Power, Jurisdiction and right, which is not by this confederation expressly delegated to the United States. . . ."* A weaker provision was substituted as part of the Bill of Rights, almost as an afterthought, and certainly as a concession "to remove the fears & quiet the apprehensions" raised first by Massachusetts and then by several other states. In any event, it was added after eleven states had already adopted the new Constitution. It was the Tenth Amendment, providing: *"The powers not delegated to the United States by the Constitution, nor prohibited by it to the States, are reserved to the States respectively, or to the people."*

The relative import of this amendment, in the thinking of

the majority at the time, can be grasped better when it is remembered that Article VI of the Constitution had been no afterthought or effort to ease the opposition of representatives from several states. The Article was the supremacy clause, the crux of the conversion from the Articles of Confederation to the Constitution:

This Constitution of the Laws of the United States which shall be made in Pursuance thereof; and all Treaties made, or which shall be made, under the Authority of the United States, shall be the supreme Law of the Land; and the Judges in every State shall be bound thereby, any Thing in the Constitution or the Laws of any State to the Contrary notwithstanding.

The intention was clear; the whole should be stronger than the sum of the parts. As the Beards summarized it:

Respecting the sovereignty, freedom, and independence of the states, as such, the Constitution contained not a word, and what it did to the pretensions of the states to full sovereignty stood out boldly in the lines imposing restraints on their powers. The announcement that the Constitution and federal laws were to be supreme over all state actions conflicting with them was unmistakable in its brevity and import. . . . Its critics understood this at the time and history to come validated the fact.[1]

The Constitution was not sent to state legislatures for ratification. Rather it was directed to separately called state conventions in the belief that the existing state government leadership might not accept such a radical shift in the role of the national government. While the conventions in Delaware, New Jersey, and Georgia voted unanimously in favor, the final acceptance came only after extensive debate. In five states, enough to have rejected the Constitution, the vote was very close. In Massachusetts, ratification came by a margin of 19 votes out of 355, and in New Hampshire by 11 votes in a total of 103. In Virginia, there was a margin of only 10 votes, and only 3 in New York. Even after the Bill of Rights was added, ratification came in Rhode Island by only 2 votes.

It was, however, ratified. It did change radically the dominant position of the states. No longer was this a country with independent states bound loosely in the fellowship of a confederation. Successive events have further weakened the relative position of the states. They have never been the same.

Even the final referee of what had been and had not been reserved to the states by the Tenth Amendment was to be at the national level. Article III provided:

"The judicial Power of the United States shall be vested in one supreme Court, and in such inferior Courts as the Congress may from time to time ordain and establish. . . . The judicial Power shall extend in all Cases, in Law and Equity, arising under this Constitution . . ."

The John Marshall Supreme Court, in a series of decisions covering the first quarter of the nineteenth century, established the U.S. Supreme Court as the final arbiter in crucial matters between the states and the national government. In its interpretation of this relationship, the Marshall Court defined the supremacy clause as meaning that the states could not interfere with the functioning of the national government, and that federal action, be it statute, treaty, court decision, or authorized administrative act, must prevail over state action.

Other events have shifted and shrunk the power of the individual state. South Carolina's attempt to nullify the tariff acts passed by Congress in the late 1820s and early 1830s led President Jackson and the Congress to reassert the predominant national authority. The individual state was rebuffed in its assumption of authority to reject or nullify an act of Congress.

The Civil War removed the ultimate resort of the individual state, secession. And in its wake, the three Civil War amendments established "national supremacy more firmly by their own words," while conferring "on Congress the power to enforce these Amendments by its legislation. Because Congress has used this power very little, it has been left largely to the Courts, and especially to the Supreme Court. . . ." [2]

The Sixteenth Amendment, ratified by all but six states,[3] gave to the national government in 1913 what was to become the most powerful advantage of all, the income tax. Money is the source of power in government, and has enabled the national government to enter and influence even those fields of responsibility reserved to the states by the Tenth Amendment.

World War I expanded the scope of the national government, and afterward left a residue of activity and dormant power in numerous fields. Thus our federalism has been worked out over the years, with each generation modifying the federal-state relationship as the problems of the day seemed to demand.

Then in the early 1930s, the depression all but submerged the states. The economic collapse was so massive the states could not feed the hungry or find jobs for the unemployed. The states had no means for boosting the economy or saving the banks.

It was hard to understate the need for action. The national income was less than half of what it had been four short years before. Nearly thirteen million Americans—about one-quarter of the labor force—were desperately seeking jobs. The machinery for sheltering and feeding the unemployed was breaking down everywhere under the growing burden. And a few hours before, in the early morning of the inauguration, every bank in America had locked its doors. It was now not just a matter of staving off hunger. It was a matter of staving off violence, even (at least some so thought) revolution.[4]

It mattered not that the states could not be held responsible for the economic collapse of the nation. The blame lay with the national government, but the people turned to the national government as the one to reverse its field and correct its previous errors, and more pointedly, the one in which strength for recovery could be found.

The depression of the 1930s forced the nation to reach back for all its historic powers in political, wartime, constitutional, and fiscal experiences, and to convert them to massive action across the nation. As a number of emergencies in the 1780s removed the first layer of retained state sovereignty, so the depression of the 1930s peeled off all the other layers right down to the core.

Out of the ordeal of the depression came damaging blows to the states. From the viewpoint of the efficacy of state government, the states lost their confidence, and the people their faith in the states; the news media became cynical, the political scientists became neglectful, and the critics became harsh.

"Is the state the appropriate instrumentality for the discharge of these sovereign functions?" Luther Gulick asked in 1933. "The answer is not a matter of conjecture or delicate appraisal. It is a matter of brutal record. The American State is finished. I do not predict that the States will go, but affirm that they have gone."[5]

1. Charles A. Beard and Mary R. Beard, *A Basic History of the United States*, (New York: Doubleday, Doran & Company, 1944), p. 129.
2. William Anderson, *The Nation and the States, Rivals or Partners?*, (Minneapolis: University of Minnesota Press, 1955), p. 106.
3. Those states which did not ratify the XVIth Amendment are: Connecticut, Florida, Pennsylvania, Rhode Island, Utah, Virginia.
4. Arthur M. Schlesinger, Jr., *The Coming of the New Deal*, (Boston: Houghton Mifflin Company, 1959), p. 3.
5. Luther C. Gulick, "Reorganization of the State," *Civil Engineering*, (August, 1933), pp. 420–421.

CHAPTER IV

The Failures of the States

Harold Laski, in a famous attack on the states, declared:

> . . . the epoch of federalism is over. . . . It is insufficiently positive in character; it does not provide for sufficient rapidity of action; it inhibits the emergence of necessary standards of uniformity; it relies upon compacts and compromises which take insufficient account of the urgent category of time; it leaves the backward areas a restraint, at once parasitic and poisonous, on those which seek to move forward; not least, its psychological results, especially in an age of crisis, are depressing to a democracy that needs the drama of positive achievement to retain its faith.[1]

This was in 1939, as Laski interpreted the evidence all around him. He saw national government as action, and state governments as reluctance and timidity. After World War II and two postwar decades, many people think they see evidence of the same kind, but more of it. The expansion and interaction of enormous social and economic forces have brought with them new burdens. They demand governmental services, and pressures mount for an expanding governmental role.

Population is exploding and people are moving. Our people flee to the city, and from there to the suburb, and they shuttle from city to city and state to state. Their migratory habits scatter the social problems of each region throughout the nation. This movement, it is argued, converts local problems into national problems. Certainly it stimulates the demand for national action. Illinois has a stake in the kind of education its immigrating Negroes have received. California absorbs, for better or worse, the education brought by the 33,000 new citizens who move there every month. Some of them dropped out in the fourth grade, but many of them have degrees from great Midwestern universities. How can one state insist that another state improve educational standards? How can one state afford to provide higher education for those who, upon graduation, go to other states to live and produce wealth?

A game like musical chairs has been played for years in every urban area. The indigent newcomer moved into the expanding slums. Those who had thrived a little better moved to a little better housing. Each group, in turn, pushed another. The constant pressure ruptured the cities' outer bounds and spattered suburbs across recent farmland. Cities crawl toward each other and touch, enveloping towns and villages in their path. Jean Gottman coined the word "megalopolis" to define this blanket occupation of the open lands. The residents became megalopolitans.[2] Listen to the following conversation, which is not unique:

Stamford Wife: I hear you are from New York.
New York Wife: Yes, I am. Are you?
Stamford Wife: Oh, yes, we're from Stamford, Connecticut. What part of New York are you from?
New York Wife: Why, we're practically neighbors. We're from Tenafly, New Jersey.[3]

The crowding of metropolitan American life has brought with it an urgent need for schools, housing, health facilities, highways, sewer systems, water, additional fire and police protection, mass transportation, and airport construction. All of these are demands on government, and if the states cannot provide the help the local government turns to Washington.

The pressures that explode the city limits leave a vacuum that crumbles the foundations of the inner city. A look at our leading cities finds none without its share of crowded and grimy housing, smelly air, children with no place to play, garbage and rats as the flora and fauna, a rising crime rate, the blackboard jungle, and too many cars, trucks, and taxis jamming and screeching. Who is responsible? The inhabitants of the slums, the city citizens of neighborhoods not yet blighted, or all residents of the total metropolitan area? Have not the states been unwilling to spend money, or make plans, or to do anything much to prevent this decay?

Because the states set the ground rules for local government, it is difficult for state government to dodge the accusing finger of municipal havoc. Among other failings, the states have been slow to cede to the cities adequate powers to tax, zone surrounding areas, regulate housing, provide or require mass transportation, and acquire open space. The states control the municipal dividing lines, and there is no logic, rhyme, or reason in the present crosshatch patterns of local government. Either the local influence against shifting city and suburban lines is too great, or the state legislature is not concerned. The states, not the cities, have the authority and position to deal with one another when a megalopolis straddles their boundaries.

If cities spill across state lines, so do smog and smoke and dirty rivers. How can one state remove the filth in the air and water that come from another state? To what expense will one state go to preserve the freshness of the water flowing to another? For example, the biggest amount of air pollution in St. Louis comes from East St. Louis, which happens to be in Illinois. What can St. Louis do? What does Illinois care? Or, to put it less cynically, what are the political pressures in Illinois to do something about making St. Louisans breathe easier? New Jersey gets much of its smoke blowing south from New York City where Consolidated Edison is still allowed to burn bituminous coal to generate electric power. What can New Jersey do? In New York, it was discovered that the prevailing winds from northern New Jersey bring the industrial fumes straight east to Manhattan. What can New York do? Jurisdictions stop at the boundaries drawn in colonial days, but the problems do not.

All this has brought many to contend that mobility, the press and spillover of population, and boundary-crossing problems make states obsolete. Because the states have not been alert to these needs, the municipal officials try to reach around them to the national government, and many federal officials try to write states, as such, out of national programs. Most of the metropolitan mayors contend that state governments have been deaf and blind, and that this now entitles them to a nonstop ticket to the national government. Therefore the mayors have established a Washington office to plead their cause and lobby for their interest, much as any trade association does.

If the people in the cities are impatient with the states because of urban problems, the farmers and the inhabitants of dwindling small towns are disappointed in the services from the states. The responsibility of the state does not stop where the last suburb sprawls into the countryside. Urbanization raises the concomitant problem of declining population in rural areas. Often, after earnest efforts to educate its children, the rural community looks up to see its youth following their education to the city. A declining population leads to a declining local tax base. The per-capita costs of services go up as population goes down. The city problems have their counterparts in the country, where the state is charged with finding the means to support schools, roads, and other governmental services for which there are not adequate local taxes. Small communities typically cry out that the state is neglecting them, while the city dwellers respond that the rural folk are getting more than they pay for. The states are blamed for letting them both down.

If the states have failed to provide adequate state revenues to aid local government, they have also been slow to straighten out the inequitable and jumbled administration of local property taxes. Tax valuations are frequently unrealistic and unfair. Most states require, theoretically, that assessments be uniform, but in too many states equalization of valuations is not required or not enforced. Assessments vary from community to community. In New Jersey (before it was corrected) the assessed valuations were found to vary from 16 to 56 per cent of true value, in Pennsylvania from 20 per cent to 78 per cent, and in Washington from 13 to 38 per cent. In states which receive a portion of the property tax collections, "there is positive encouragement to competitive under-assessment as means of minimizing local contributions. Half the states distribute grants-in-aid on formulas based on local wealth as evidenced by the assessed values. This system penalizes correct assessment and rewards under-assessment." [4]

Most states have not developed a candid state-wide tax policy of their own. The failure is partly a result of competition between states. National taxes are not competitive; state taxes are. People preparing to retire, all other considerations being equal, choose a state where the tax on securities and inheritance is minimal. Of more drastic influence is the blustery competition for industry. Since World War II the states have contested fiercely for jobs and income for their people. They should. But this rivalry makes them supersensitive to any new tax, especially one that touches industry. Some states advertise favored tax positions for new plants, and all states have industry hunters who present convincingly the tax advantages awaiting a prospective industry. In a glass case in the middle of the airport terminal in Salt Lake

City is a display with the caption: "Utah is a freeport state. No property tax on inventory held for out-of-state shipment. If stored in California, the tax would add more than 20 per cent to your storage cost each year." In North Carolina, a reluctant legislature authorized in 1967 the issuance of tax-free revenue bonds to finance new industrial buildings because 32 other states have done so. Officials in Maryland complain that North Carolina should impose a cigarette tax so Marylanders will not avoid the Maryland tax by purchasing cigarettes by the case in North Carolina. For the same reason the governor of California urges "the California delegation to seek an amendment to the present federal law regarding interstate shipments of cigarettes, so that our merchants will be protected from mail-order competition. . . ."[5]

There is no generally accepted philosophy of state taxation. Many maintain, given the competitive nature of state activities, that states will never be able to reach a wise tax philosophy, and are doomed to become more and more dependent on the federal government for revenue. The state taxpayers have no idea what they should expect, and therefore frequently refuse to tolerate an essential tax structure. In Nebraska, in the 1966 November election, the voters defeated a proposal to add a state income tax, and at the same time voted to abolish the state property tax. The votes left the state with no major tax sources, but it is only fair to add that this cleared the way for a better plan of taxation later adopted. This lack of accepted tax philosophy and the widespread misunderstanding on the part of the voters cause legislators in many states to impose special and hidden taxes which, they feel, will stir the least political reaction. Perhaps as one New England legislator told us, "The only way we could get a realistic and workable tax program in this state is if the legislature from Oregon sat in our capitol and made our tax laws, and our legislature sat in Oregon and did the same for them."

There are a number of government duties the states cannot be expected to assume. Only the national government, in our mobile society, can enact and administer a program of social security, and regulate interstate transportation and the use of television channels. These functions, along with many others, obviously are interstate.

In other matters, it was not the interstate nature of the problem that brought in the national government. The national government got into hospital construction because state and local governments, for whatever reasons, had neglected hospitals. The national government came to the general support of education (mostly in the guise of national defense and help for disadvantaged children) because the states were not spending enough to reach the goals most Americans considered imperative. The national government became involved in slum clearance because the state and local governments did not know what to do, or if they did, thought they did not have the money.

State constitutions, or most of them drafted in the late nineteenth century, have stifled the vitality of state government. Those which have not been revised contain unusually excessive operational detail, bad for many reasons that David Fellman points out:

It makes temporary matters permanent. It deprives state legislatures and local governments of desirable flexibility and diminishes their sense of responsibility. It encourages the search for methods of evading constitutional provisions and thus tends to debase our sense of constitutional morality. . . . It hinders action in time of special stress or emergency. It stands in the way of healthy progress. It blurs distinction between constitutional and statute law, to the detriment of both. It creates badly written instruments full of obsolete, repetitious, misleading provisions. Above all, it confuses the public. . . .[6]

A constitution, in the words of Justice Cardozo, should provide "not rules for the passing hour, but principles for an expanding future." [7]

The South Carolina Constitution defines what shall constitute a durable hard-surface road in Greenville. South Dakota's Constitution sets the debt limit at $100,000 unless the state is invaded. The Oklahoma Constitution requires the teaching of home economics in all public schools. Texas provides for the election of the inspector of hides and animals. Kansas and Nevada require election of the state printer.

The Model State Constitution (prepared by the National Municipal League) is 12,000 words. New Jersey's, rewritten in 1947, contains 12,500 words; Vermont, characteristically, gets along very well with 4,840 words. The Louisiana Constitution is 236,000 words, at least half as long as *Gone with the Wind*. The Alabama and California constitutions are each about the length of the book you are reading. Seven more have more than thirty thousand words. But verbosity is not of itself a disadvantage. The hindrances to the efficiency of state government arise from the details, and from the necessity sometimes to ignore constitutional provisions in order to assure the day-to-day operation of government. It would be far better to amend and modernize the Constitution, for as Adlai Stevenson remarked in discussing the point, "when we lose respect for constitutional government, we lose respect for democracy." [8]

Generally, too many constitutions require the election of too many state officials. Forgetting the printers, inspectors of hides, and surveyors, too many officers of cabinet rank are elected by the people under specific requirements of the state constitution. It is argued that this holds government closer to the people, that the people have the last word. But in practice it simply is not so; the people barely know the offices exist, and cannot possibly keep up with their activities and performances.

In Utah, the constitution requires government by troika.

The governor is required to make all decisions regarding the expenditure of state funds (except for some items of compensation) in concurrence with one of two other elected state officials, the attorney general or the secretary of state. In New Hampshire the constitution provides for a separately elected council of five, which can veto various executive decisions and must approve all appointments.

Oregon has a board of control, made up of the governor, state treasurer, and secretary of state, who meet to control the insane asylums, mental hospitals, prisons, and institutions for the blind and the deaf, often delaying even the most cut-and-dried administrative decisions. In Florida the governor shares the executive authority of the state with six others: the superintendent of public instruction, the secretary of state, the attorney general, the treasurer, the comptroller, and the commissioner of agriculture. All are independently elected, and all have other specific duties subordinate to the executive, yet they fix the budget, approve budget transfers, and serve as ex-officio members of boards administering many of the major functions of the state government. The composition of these boards varies, and when the governor is a member of a board, his vote is equal to that of any other member, with two minor exceptions.

Few institutions are as balkanized as the executive branch of state government. William H. Young said, "The American governorship was conceived in mistrust and born in a strait jacket, the creature of revolutionary assemblies." [9] This fact has, for many years, put state government at a disadvantage.

"The story is told that when William Hooper went home after attending the North Carolina Convention in 1776 and was asked how much power was given to the governor, he replied: 'Just enough to sign the receipt for his salary.'" [10] The governor of North Carolina today does not have the veto power, generally for the same reasons.

This diffusion of the governor's authority hinders and

stymies the states. Imagine the bewilderment if the President's cabinet were elected by the people. It would be impossible to pinpoint responsibility; it would be difficult to know who was doing what; no policy decision could be reached unless the President compromised and conceded to obtain the necessary agreement. The decision would not be the President's, but the public would have no way of knowing whose it was.

The same fears that caused the revolutionary assemblies to hamstring the governor's office caused the early opposition to a strong national executive. There was no President under the Articles of Confederation. History has now demonstrated the leadership inherent in the strong presidential office with organization and authority commensurate with the duties of the office. History has also demonstrated the difficulty in developing strong leadership from the governor's office. Almost no governor in the country has authority that even approaches his responsibility. The state constitutions fairly adequately prevent the governor from committing evil. That was perhaps the intent. They also hinder his attempt to pursue excellence.

In judging the achievements of state government, it is well to remember that the people have not wanted a strong governor; they have not been willing to trust the man they elect at the polls. They have not been willing to put the authority and the implements in the hands of the man called on by them to lead, to care for their cities and towns, to promote the schools for their children, to eliminate slums and smog and highway congestion, and to represent them in dealing with Washington. They have been willing to have a strong executive of their national government, but unwilling to provide the power necessary for the executive of the state government.

Not only is this true in the constitutional provisions, it has been repeated over the years by statutory enactment as state legislatures created new boards and commissions independent or substantially independent of the governor's direction and supervision. When he first took office in 1965, Governor Daniel J. Evans of Washington called a cabinet meeting. Sixty showed; he reorganized his cabinet procedures.

Our questionnaires to the governors on the subject of the role of boards and commissions got a vigorous response. Sample comments reflect the attitudes of the men responsible for the administration of states:

A ROCKY MOUNTAIN STATE: ". . . A governor finds it difficult enough to bring his policies to bear on a single administrator; when confronted with a reluctant board, whose membership can be changed only through death, expiration of term, or for cause, the situation, to say the least, becomes exasperating."

A NEW ENGLAND STATE: "The reason for gubernatorial loss of control is the fragmentation of administration. It makes responsible management impossible. It separates responsibility and accountability from authority."

A MIDWESTERN STATE: ". . . there seems to be no question . . . that executive and administrative type agencies headed by boards and commissions tend to give more influence to the staffs of those agencies and to the private interest groups which are affected by the activities of that agency."

A STATE WITH A NEW CONSTITUTION: "Boards and commissions should be utilized when the function to be exercised is basically regulatory, quasi-judicial, or quasi-legislative in nature. I do not believe that the boards or commissions should be entrusted with essentially executive duties of the operation and day-to-day administration."

As it now stands, the governor cannot always be held accountable for failures even when they are directly his. It is difficult to prove who was supposed to be doing what.

People do not have very much faith in their states. Constitutional revisions have been generally unsuccessful. The very people who complain about the weakness of the states have a compulsion to keep them weak. Perhaps it is as one governor said to me: "Don't talk about making the states stronger. Stay away from that word. The people don't want any government to be strong. They can't do anything about the federal government, but they can keep the states weak in comparison, and will do so on almost any given occasion."

Not only are governors weak in comparison to their responsibilities, but so are state legislatures. Both have to combat numerous predatory foes. State legislatures have never been provided adequate staff assistance. More accurately, they have never provided for themselves the clerical and research support they need, and this fact is a reflection of public attitudes. Keeping state legislatures ineffective does not protect the public. It only helps special interests dominate the legislature.

Lobbyists are now legion in Washington, but they have always flocked to state legislatures. Railroads ran many a state for decades. So did power companies. In Montana, Anaconda Copper exercised disproportionate influence; in Illinois and Florida, the race tracks; in Wyoming, the cattlemen's association; in Louisiana, the oil companies; and in Connecticut, the drug industry and the insurance companies. A number of people in Arizona informed me that until about 1950 the state budget was blue-penciled in the out-of-state home office of a mining company before it was submitted to the legislature for approval.

Frank Trippett contends that the true constituency of the state legislatures is the business community.[11] This concept has been another factor in the transfer of governmental functions to the national government. The general constituency of the state legislature often has been too small to provide strong resistance to special interests. When the mining states could not resist the local pressures of the mining companies, it took a number of scandalous disasters and national legislation to assure safer mining laws. When the state of California could not resist adequately the lumber interests, it took the national government to save the redwoods. Many states couldn't resist the industrial interests, and it took the national government to enact adequate child-labor laws. Trippett concludes:

The state legislature in short has stood in fact for government closest to all the people except those who live in villages, towns, cities, sewer districts, recreation districts, zoning districts, water districts, judicial circuits, counties—and states.[12]

Many officials elected to run the states do not draw from their constituencies, for whatever reason or complex set of reasons, the confidence needed for state leadership. Far too many officials fall back into a frame of mind "early American" in orientation and provincial in outlook. They spend more money each year, but often are forced to do so in order to match funds from the the national government. They too easily follow the lead of others, grudgingly, rather than leading and innovating. Rather than seeking to do something about the legitimate causes of discontent, they are too inclined to oppose the evidences of change within their own boundaries—urbanization, economic emancipation, and increased civil rights and liberties. Their inclination is to see the problems of social welfare as something for the individual and not society to work out. Urban problems "spring from unhealthy soil, even from the misdeeds, of the city . . . [an] unnatural and unwanted issue of American growth. . . ."[13] In this frame of mind they rationalize that these and similar problems are too complex for the states to handle—resources are inadequate, there are too many problems, and it is not the states' proper role to tackle every problem. This habit of thought results "in a hard-bitten and almost uniform conservatism: What has been done over a period of years can continue to be done, but what is new and different must be regarded with suspicion." [14]

These attitudes reflect the constituencies of the states, or many state leaders must think so. Maybe the structures of state governments, the traditions, the constitutional limitations, the narrowness of the state legislator's individual electorate, or the legalistic dampers on state leadership have an additional influence. In any event, the people have increasingly turned from state government and have insisted on looking elsewhere: to the national Congress, the Supreme Court, the federal bureaucracy. The people seem to conclude that the state vehicle is not so driveable as the federal vehicles.

The states, or so it has been contended for one hundred and fifty years, have failed to advance with their citizens into the modern world. In an exhibit of the Nebraska Historical Society this bit of nostalgia appeared:

> Fittingly, the beginnings of our territory were turbulent. Armed with Colt revolvers and Bowie knives, our legislators sat at their school-boy desks prepared for all differences of opinion.

While the Nebraska legislature has changed most constructively, about the only self-imposed change in the representative government of some states is that revolvers and knives are no longer standard equipment. At the end of 1962, twenty-seven states had not redistricted their legislatures in twenty-five years, and eight states had not redistricted in more than fifty years. Pleas to reapportion were generally dismissed by state legislatures. Finally, the pressures built until the Supreme Court acted, and this has fanned the old complaints that state legislatures are not willing to meet their responsibilities.

The right of states to serve the needs of their citizens is an honorable and historic position, but one difficulty is that selfish interests have sought to parade the appeal of states' rights to screen their opposition to needed programs and policies. The former governor of Florida, Leroy Collins, in a symposium several years ago, exposed this particular technique:

Minimum wages are a good example. Those economic interests which have opposed—in the name of states' rights—every single effort at the federal level to provide American citizens assurance of decent minimum wages have not encouraged the state governments to provide such. It is not really "federal encroachment" they oppose: it is minimum wages.[15]

The authentic doctrine of states' rights, supported by a commitment to states' responsibilities, has often been misused. Some men dodge behind the banner of states' rights to avoid controversial issues; others use it to camouflage their opposition to all government; still others cloak injustice in its folds. "States' rights" is a tattered ensign, ripped and torn by those who seek to rally support for their own selfish ends. They have undermined the states' rights they seek, and are a greater hindrance to the states they claim to save than any other hurdle on the road back to more responsible and responsive state government.

Because many groups and people have encountered evasion of duty by the state, they have felt that they had no choice but to try the road to Washington. The trek to Washington could have been expected, for government is not static. Woodrow Wilson wrote that government is not a machine, but a living thing:

It falls, not under the theory of the universe, but under the theory of organic life. It is accountable to Darwin, not to Newton. It is modified by its environment, necessitated by its tasks, shaped to its functions by the sheer pressure of life.[16]

The recalcitrance that marks many of the states certainly does not mark them all, but timidity, reluctance, and obsolescence are nationwide. When twentieth-century growth began to overtake us, the machinery of state government was outmoded, revenue resources were outstripped, and the state executive was denied the tools of leadership long supplied the President of the United States.

The states have fumbled for solutions, but they fumbled within the old framework and with outdated concepts of government. Too many voters have failed to understand that state government can no longer be merely a regulating and holding operation; that if their states do not guide and channel the growth they cannot take their proper place in the world of the future. In "An Anniversary Talk with Huntley and Brinkley," Huntley expressed the conventional opinion:

How we govern ourselves is still up in the air, too. The state legislatures and the governors keep yelling that they should be solving problems at their own levels, but they can't do it; they're just not equipped for it.

And Brinkley added:

States are pretty much disappearing as a political force. They're almost through. I think in another generation they will be, politically speaking, just about insignificant.[17]

To this might be added the doleful prediction of Senator Everett McKinley Dirksen: "The only people interested in state boundaries will be Rand-McNally." [18]

"State government is at a crossroads," writes Senator Joseph D. Tydings:

For a hundred years, the states have been losing ground to the federal government and they have sunk into lower and lower repute in the eyes of the electorate. In recent years, they have been increasingly by-passed as federal funds to cure urban ills go directly to our cities. Unless the states act decisively to shake off their lethargy and meet the challenges of this decade and the next, they will wither on the vine. This is, I believe, their last chance.[19]

The states have gained a bad reputation, although it is not entirely justified. If the states do have a role important to the future of the citizens of the United States, and they do, then the challenge to the state leaders is to shape a new character which by action and results will establish a new reputation. Part of the challenge belongs to the voting citizens, for they have the most to gain—or lose.

1. Harold J. Laski, "The Obsolescence of Federalism," *New Republic,* (May 3, 1939), p. 367.
2. Jean Gottman, *Megalopolis,* (New York: The Twentieth Century Fund, 1961).
3. Ben J. Wattenberg with Richard M. Scammon, *This U.S.A.,* (Garden City, New York: Doubleday & Company, 1965), p. 72.
4. Roger A. Freeman, "What Ails Property Tax?" *National Municipal Review,* XLIV, (November, 1955), p. 509.
5. Tax Message of Ronald Reagan, Governor of California, transmitted to the California Legislature, March 8, 1967, p. 10.
6. David Fellman, "What Should a State Constitution Contain?," in W. Brooke Graves, (ed.), *Major Problems in State Constitutional Revision,* (Chicago: Public Administration Service, 1960), p. 146.
7. Benjamin Cardozo, *The Nature of the Judicial Process,* (New Haven: Yale University Press, 1921), p. 83.
8. Address of Adlai E. Stevenson, Governor of Illinois, before the Merchants and Manufacturers Club, Merchandise Mart, Chicago, March 16, 1949.
9. William H. Young, "The Development of the Governorship," *State Government,* (Summer, 1952), p. 178.
10. Robert S. Rankin, *The Government and Administration of North Carolina,* (New York: Thomas Y. Crowell Company, 1955), p. 75.
11. Frank Trippett, *The States—United They Fell,* (New York: The World Publishing Company, 1967), p. 33.
12. *Ibid.,* p. 231.
13. Roscoe C. Martin, *The Cities and the Federal System.* (New York: Atherton Press, 1965), p. 78.
14. *Ibid.*
15. Leroy Collins in "The Mazes of Government," (Santa Barbara, California: Center for the Study of Democratic Institutions, 1964), p. 3.
16. Woodrow Wilson, *Constitutional Government in the United States,* (New York: Columbia University Press, 1908), p. 56.
17. James F. Fixx, "An Anniversary Talk with Huntley and Brinkley," *McCall's* (October, 1966), p. 176.
18. *The New York Times,* August 8, 1965, Section IV, p. 2.
19. Joseph D. Tydings, "Reform Is Possible," *National Civic Review,* Vol. LVI, (January, 1967), p. 11.

CHAPTER V

Attempts Toward Improvement

Finding fault with state government is nothing new. Those responsible for improving state government have been served acid by the commentators. "The real blemishes in the system of state government are all found in the composition or conduct of the legislatures," observed one. Inferiority in "knowledge, skill, and sometimes also conscience," was his appraisal. He added that their other faults included "improvidence in matters of finance," as well as "want of proper methods for dealing with local and special bills." [1]

This comment appeared in James Bryce's *The American Commonwealth,* the first truly comprehensive dissection of the American society after the Civil War. These words were written in 1888.

And now, nearly eighty years later, another critic blasted the states by attacking the legislatures.

Anyone writing of the state as an instrument of government must write of the legislature. To indict the states is to indict the legislatures . . . that legislatures are inefficient and corrupt, that they procrastinate on public business while habitually kowtowing to private economic interests, that legislators get drunk and disorderly and consort with ladies procured by avaricious lobbyists, that they line their own pockets, scratch their own backs and roll their own logs—all the while stamping out progressive legislation in the name of protecting their constituents. [2]

My experiences do not bear out these harsh observations.

I suppose this kind of muckraking serves a purpose. It may stir to action those who have not had much concern for taking part in state government. But while these charges might have a good effect, they are simply not an accurate report. They are strong and the culprit is named. But does the total implication constitute a true bill? First, it assumes that the ills of one branch of state government, the legislature, even if the charges are true, visit upon the whole of state government an aura of negligence or neglect, if not evil. Second, it generalizes from the particular; drunken legislators indict all legislators; corruption in one means all are corrupt; one inefficient and backward legislature stands for forty-nine other similar legislatures. Third, it assumes the states stand at the bar as being the only nonresponsive and irresponsible units of government.

Of course states are not the only culprits. Our history has recorded neglect and a lack of responsibility from the local recorder's court to the White House. There is no particular locus of ultimate wisdom and devotion to duty in governmental affairs.

Nor is it a fact that legislative corruption is widespread. It is easy to repeat an old cliché, grasping at every individual infraction to reinforce its truth; but the ancient cliché that legislators are more corrupt than other men doesn't apply to the vast majority of state legislators. I have known and met with legislators from almost every state. I have worked with many of them on committees. I have served in a state legislature. I can remember three or four who did the general reputation of the body no good, but also I can think of many more of similar ilk in the national Congress. This statement doesn't condemn either the Congress or the legislature. The overwhelming majority in both places are conscientious and diligent, and attempt to reflect what they believe best for their states and country. They are not corrupt as institutions, as groups, as legislatures. Only a handful are questionable as individuals. Certainly these charges do an injustice to the 95 per cent who serve honorably. No corruption is justified, however, and perhaps Trippett's recounting of the old evils will help eliminate them.

James Q. Wilson, after a careful analysis of recent Commonwealth of Massachusetts Crime Commission reports, suggests that a major, initial cause of corruption is the very structure of fragmented state government.

What the founders have put asunder, the politicians must join together if anything is to be accomplished. Because each branch can—and sometimes does—paralyze the other, American government "is so constituted that it cannot be carried on without corruption." The boss, the machine, the political party, the bagmen— all these operate . . . to concert the action of legally independent branches of government through the exchange of favors. The solution to corruption, if this is its cause, is to bring these various departments together formally and constitutionally. . . . [But] the states have rarely been subjected to the kinds of reforms which have gradually centralized formal authority in the hands of a professional city manager or a single strong mayor.[3]

Or, for that matter, in the hands of the President of the United States.

If this analysis is correct, what have the states done to set their houses in order? What are they doing now about the structural faults which compel inefficiency and may lead to corruption?

After Massachusetts' experience with the Crime Commission, the people of the state did take the first significant steps toward organizational reform. Generally considered to have had one of the worst structures of state government in the country, Massachusetts is now becoming a pacesetter for improvement in structural and constitutional reform. By initiative vote in 1964, the people of Massachusetts removed most of the appointive power (with the exception of judges) from the Executive Council and placed it in the hands of the governor. In addition, the state officers were given four-year terms beginning in 1966. Former Governor Endicott Peabody told me in a personal interview that

These amendments to the constitution have considerably overhauled the executive in Massachusetts and given him real authority to match his responsibility. I think that the outlook for the long run—in giving Massachusetts effective government, in restoring the confidence of the alienated voter, in eliminating corruption—is tremendous. Ten years from now constitutional reforms will be looked upon as doing more to clean up corruption in the state than ten crime commissions put end to end.

We are currently engaged in the fourth wave of reform in the American states. The first followed a 1912 report by President Taft's Federal Economy and Efficiency Commission, which recommended adoption of an executive budget system for the federal government. After that report (which was not followed at the national level for several years), twenty-six of the states reorganized, many of them comprehensively.[4]

The states were shown the way in 1917, "when Illinois, under the leadership of Governor Frank O. Lowden, adopted the first comprehensive plan of administrative reorganization."[5] Under this plan, "administratively and politically, the Illinois governor ascended to new eminence and influence."[6] Other states followed, including New York under the leadership of Governor Alfred E. Smith. The National Municipal League turned its attentions to the problems of the states. In 1921 the League published "A Model State Constitution" which set as a guideline for the states "a centralized plan of State organization, headed by the governor, a single-house legislature, and unified court structure.[7]

The second wave of state reorganization followed the appointment of another federal commission by President Franklin D. Roosevelt in 1937. Over a dozen states undertook reorganization. In the quarter of a century during which these two waves of reform occurred, "every state in the Union has at one time or another . . . considered the matter of administrative reorganization." [8]

Eleven states attempted "to make the governor in fact, as well as in theory, the responsible chief executive of the state." Almost all states tried to integrate their numerous boards and agencies into a few orderly departments "to locate responsibility for administrative action or inaction." Others aimed at having an independent legislative audit, removing boards and commissions from administrative responsibilities, establishing an appointed governor's cabinet, and setting up other procedures which aid coordination of effort in the executive branch. Reforms were also undertaken of the legislative and the judicial branches.[9]

The third great wave was stimulated by the first and second Hoover commissions, established under the Truman and Eisenhower administrations to recommend ways to reorganize the executive branch of the national government. There were many "'little Hoover Commissions' in states and cities, indicating that keeping state government, or any government, organized for action is a never-ending task.

"'Concentration of authority and responsibility,' 'functional integration,' 'direct lines of responsibility,' 'grouping of related services,' 'elimination of overlapping and duplication,' and 'need for coordination' echoed through state capitols. . . ." [10]

And now in 1967 we find that over half the states are attempting constitutional and administrative revisions and that study commissions in many other states are preparing recommendations. In the 1966 elections alone, voters in fourteen states considered amendments to reorganize the legislatures; in eight states they voted on changes in the executive branch; in thirteen states, on judicial improvement; in four states, on other basic constitutional amendments; and in eleven states, on revision in the relations between state and local governments. Not all efforts toward reform were successful, nor were they all in the same direction—but an impulse toward change is clearly present.

On the legislative side alone much ferment is apparent as the impact of the U.S. Supreme Court's decisions on reapportionment is felt. State after state has drawn and redrawn the boundaries of its legislative representatives' districts. Some observers feel that the greatest impact of reapportionment will be subtle. They see state departments and agencies beginning to become more responsive to urban areas in order to defend budget requests before reapportioned legislatures. New blood is being infused into the system. Some critics are unkind enough to say that the state legislatures are merely exchanging suburban reactionaries for rural reactionaries, young fogies for old fogies. But legislative reform is not going to work out this way. Almost everywhere earnest attempts are under way to remove legislative encumbrances and to develop public support for a more capable legislative process in the states. We would make a mistake, however, if we assume that structural change is the panacea. It will take structure, but more important it will take leadership and a fresh attitude.

Reform will follow a change in the atmosphere of government. In the 1960s I detect a sense of direction and the excitement of action in our American states. There is a new consciousness of the possibilities for achievement. Reapportionment, the accumulating activity of the national government, and the developing confidence of the states in their ability to improve have combined to move the governors to new ventures, to new hopes, and to new determination.

The success of each wave of reform has been limited by the acceptance of the people. Thus the success of the present wave, probably the most concerted and general effort yet, lies in the willingness and the desire of the people to encourage and to push for the necessary changes and reforms. For all of this century and before, the need for shoring up the foundations of state government has been pointed out to the people. The people have been reluctant and slow, all the while permitting the expansion of the strengths of the national government, over which they have less control and in which fewer restraints were built.

The extent of change and improvement today will be determined by how urgent the people believe the cause to be.

1. James Bryce, *The American Commonwealth*, rev. ed., (London and New York: The Macmillan Company, 1906), Vol. I, p. 550.
2. Frank Trippett, *The States—United They Fell*, (New York: The World Publishing Company, 1967), pp. 2–3.
3. James Q. Wilson, "Corruption: The Shame of the States," *Public Interest*, No. 2. (Winter, 1966), pp. 31, 35.
4. A. E. Buck, *The Reorganization of State Governments in the United States*, (New York: Columbia University Press, 1938), pp. 7–8.
5. *Ibid.*, p. 7.
6. Herbert Kaufman, "Emerging Conflicts in the Doctrines of Public Administration," *The American Political Science Review*, Vol. L, (December, 1956), p. 1065.
7. Buck, *op. cit.*, p. 12.
8. *Ibid.*, p. 44.
9. *Ibid.*, pp. 14–28, *passim.*
10. Kaufman, *op. cit.*

CHAPTER VI

The Press and the Public

Why is it difficult to get the voters to accept reforms? The United States is so steeped in the philosophy of self-government that one would expect citizens to demand efficient, honest government, and those who champion it to be celebrated for their good works.

Sadly, this is not usually the fact, and the reason, I suspect, is that the people are not fully aware of the deficiencies or adequately informed of the need and means of correction. The 1966 elections are a good case in point. In Utah, voters said "no," by a margin in excess of five to one, to a proposal for calling a constitutional convention, and defeated the other reform measures on the ballot by margins of two or three to one. In Kentucky and West Virginia, all major proposals for government reform were defeated. Voters in Missouri rejected a proposal that would have allowed St. Louis to begin drafting a plan to establish a metropolitan government.

The difficulties in renovating moldy state institutions are many. First is a "natural" opposition to change no matter how great the need. People are hesitant to abandon familiar structures for a vague new architecture that may not be as comfortable. The burden is always on the proponents of change to convince the people of the need and, without a dramatic event to arouse popular concern, the convincing is difficult. Unless emergency or urgent need is shown, the voters will likely vote "no."

Second, there simply are not many troops to be summoned to the cause of reorganizing state government. Few can get really excited about it. It sounds dull, structural, academic. Mention constitutional reform on the campaign trail and the yawning response of the average voter will quickly set you searching for other issues. Professor Harold Norris of the Detroit College of Law recently wrote:

But it is harder for people to get excited about the question of power (who shall do it?) than about the issues and programs (what shall be done?). Power has a greater reach into the future; program is more immediate. It takes more political insight and vision to understand power than program.[1]

And this means it is more difficult to explain.

Third, some special interests have desired a weak and fragmented state government to protect their own favored positions. After the Utah elections and the overwhelming defeat of all constitutional reforms, columnist Bruce Biossat reported:

The assault was joined in, it is said, by Utah's power and mining interests, by the highway users who feared revision might allow some user taxes to go into general revenues, by Chambers of Commerce, and an organization called the Taxpayer's Association.[2]

The special irony is that the same people who always fight state reforms are usually the loudest whiners about the destruction of states' rights and the expanding power of federal government. That they are the chief contributors to the increase of that power and the inabilities of the states is overlooked in the din of their complaints against state taxes, effective state laws, and adequate executive powers.

Fourth, and perhaps the most enfeebling, the public has a negative image of state government. *Politics, politician,* and *patronage* are words to conjure up smirking public response, with dark hints of graft, nepotism, conflict of interest, and filchery. Although such hints should lend force to reform efforts, they seem, instead, to lead to cynical disinterest.

Unfortunately, the lack of public interest contributes to a lack of interest by the press as well and probably vice versa. Every newspaperman we interviewed agreed that the shallow coverage of the press distorts the over-all picture of state government activity and conveys the image of an irrelevant bureaucracy.

Many papers rely heavily on the wire services for state government coverage, but the wires, like the papers, are not able, or are not disposed, to staff their state capital bureaus with enough people to cover adequately what goes on. Only a handful of state government reporters have the technical competence to grasp the significance of many major government stories and relate them to other current or past events and social or economic changes. Newspaperman Tom Littlewood says the job of covering the statehouse requires a "detective, political scientist, and technical specialist in public administration, the law, psychology, and diverse other disciplines."[3] But a Midwestern wire-service reporter told me that "while the state government has steadily gotten more complex, our staff hasn't changed in twenty years."

Given the lack of adequate staff to cover state government, and the papers' space problems, it is only natural that much of what is reported is negative, because a newspaper may consider its primary function to be public watchdog. Within this context, background stories and in-depth analyses of significant state efforts necessarily rate a back-page snippet in comparison with the front-page stories of the antics of clowns in the legislature or the gaffes of the governor or members of his administration.

The negative image of state government, Ben Bagdikian notes, often results from the inner conflict within the newspaper publisher as educator versus businessman:

This conflict . . . feeds one of the most pernicious diseases of press treatment of government: a primitive and simplistic view of what government ought to be. It arises from the myth that the best government is the one that governs least (rather than the more rational suggestion that the best government is one that governs best). It is an attitude found on city desks and editorial conference tables which often dismiss all governmental units as white-collar families of the Mafia, the hardboiled, corner-of-the-mouth decision that "they're all a bunch of crooks," when, as a matter of fact, this is true only part of the time and in those cases the papers don't do much about it. If press vis-à-vis government is a relationship of cops-and-robbers, then it is only human that the press decides that it is not the robber. Or that it looks upon its role in reporting and commenting on state government as urging the political leadership of men who pretend to be devoted to liquidating their political function, as though public administration were a branch of the American Cancer Society.[4]

 Responsible newspapers see their role as participants in the process of citizen education, as reporter, interpreter, evaluator, and critical observer of the events and activities that touch the interests and welfare of their readers. It is difficult to estimate the influence of newspapers, for it takes many forms, but their role in the educational process is substantial; as a consequence, their role in the processes, performance, and temper of government is significant. They have, or so I contend, an accompanying responsibility. As Bagdikian says succinctly: "In most places the political system adapts to the values of the communications system."[5]

One observer in Missouri, when asked what effect reapportionment would have in his state, noted: "Well, it certainly will increase the power of the *St. Louis Post-Dispatch* in state politics." The impact can also be direct. At least one state official thinks that "papers that do a good job act as a kind of instant intelligence for government. Officials find out more about what is going on throughout government by reading the newspapers than through their own internal organizations. So when the press is bad, there is a breakdown of communications within the state itself. The muscles slacken."

On the other hand, a newspaper can have an enormous negative effect. Not one person my staff interviewed in New Hampshire failed to mention that the *Manchester Union-Leader* was considered demoralizing on state government. Many state officials said they feared personal and vindictive editorial reprisal on the front page if they took public exception to one of the paper's policies. They feel the paper has created an emotionally charged, reactionary atmosphere where new ideas are frequently not only rejected but fail to appear in print for public discussion. Thus change may be stifled simply because it is change.

Yet one cannot expect the press always to be constructive or to suggest better alternatives. Certainly it does not have the responsibility to design the reform of state government; one television commentator said at our conference, "I can tell when an egg is bad, but I can't lay one." It is important also that newspapers never become the apologists for, or captives of, any government—the uncritical purveyor of deparmental handouts or gubernatorial statements. The press tradition of suspicion and skepticism is healthy for the body politic. But undue cynicism sometimes perverts that tradition.

Having criticized the press, let us in honesty now say that state government has become less interesting to most people than the space race, the cold war, sports, movie stars, air crashes, Congress, and hallucinogenic drugs. Actually state government activities are full of human interest and drama, but state government is not going to be well presented in the press until it finds a more exciting way to present its activities.

One question remains. What responsibility does the press

have to support reform in state government? Effective support would require reporting fully and perceptively the actions, the difficulties, and the problems of state government. It would require newspapers to draw comprehensive pictures of the needs and shortages, demands and decisions, stumbling blocks and assets that are part of any government. At the same time, they would have to do the much harder job of reporting what is not happening. Newspapers would have to point out the ills which beset the states—the antiquated constitutions, the difficult tax structures, the diffusion of executive authority, and all the other handicaps to progressive state action. Who, in some forty states or more, can say he begins to understand state government by what he reads in the newspapers?

In any event, where the newspapers do prod, the people usually insist on improvement. Newspapers can create public interest to stimulate public action when they feel they have a public responsibility. Does the crumbling of the federal system seem as important to them as the crumbling of the downtown shopping area where their advertisers trade? Is urging the reform and revitalization of state government a newspaper duty, or can they be content, as objective observers, simply to chronicle its demise? I don't know. When I suggested this thought to a newsman whose chief beat is Washington, he replied, "That is not the newspapers' job. That is just another problem for state government."

Norman Isaacs, executive editor of the *Louisville Courier-Journal*, a paper that for years has reported competently on government in two states, wrote me after a conference we had on this subject. Part of the problem, he said, is technical, for governors seem not to give their press relations much thought. But "the over-all problem you posed—of how to make state government exciting and interesting enough for the press to cover fully and intelligently—continues to haunt me. I agree with you that a key factor is the personality of a governor. But it isn't enough to pin the entire responsibility on any chief executive. The problem of government is with us [the press] regardless of the man who holds a top state office." [6]

Another newsman said: "Publishers have a responsibility to the public to do more. Call it public service, if you will. Sure, state government doesn't have the glamour, but the press has the responsibility to enlighten and serve."

1. Harold Norris, "Constitutions: The Politics of Power," *The Nation*, (November 7, 1966), p. 472.
2. Bruce Biossat, Syndicated Column, Newspaper Enterprise Association, *The Durham Sun*, (North Carolina), November 28, 1966.
3. Tom Littlewood, "The Trials of Statehouse Journalism," *Saturday Review*, (December 10, 1966), p. 82.
4. Ben H. Bagdikian, "The Hometown Daily: Afghanistan vs. State House," unpublished paper prepared for A Study of American States, (September, 1965), p. 9.
5. *Ibid.*, p. 11.
6. Letter from Norman E. Isaacs, Vice President and Executive Editor, *The Courier-Journal*, Louisville, Kentucky, September 15, 1965.

CHAPTER VII

The States Have Done Much

The argument that the states are anachronisms and need to be replaced by more relevant governmental bodies is a facile conclusion for those who are dismayed by the disorder of American government. This is a classroom solution. But the stubborn facts are that the states do exist, have a fairly strong political base, and will be here for the foreseeable future. There are also promises of good in the states which should bring the eager critic to a more cheerful acceptance of the facts.

The states are the focal points in our system of political parties, with presidential campaigns as more or less quadrennial coalitions of state political structures. The candidates for president and vice-president must key their efforts on a state-by-state basis to win support at the national party conventions. They are picked finally by state delegations on a roll call of the states. A state-by-state approach to campaigning is necessary to win the electoral votes of sufficient states to be elected.

In addition, U.S. congressmen and senators are products of the state political systems, usually are responsive to the state political party leadership, and are frequently influenced by governors and state legislatures.

The states have always occupied and still do occupy a strong constitutional position in the nation. The states created the Constitution, if not the Union, and retain constitutional rights and obligations which make them far more than subdivisions or creatures of the national government. Each state has two senators, so that the smallest or most thinly populated state may have full rights in the family of states. This position of equality is protected by the constitutional provision "that no State, without its Consent, shall be deprived of its equal Suffrage in the Senate."

In governmental duties, the states bear primary responsibility for many traditional functions, including education, health, and highways. They exercise considerable regulatory powers. In addition, the states also contribute funds and serve as the administrative vehicles for most of such federal grant-in-aid programs as vocational rehabilitation, welfare, and civil defense.

The states directly and daily conduct a vast amount of essential governmental business, touching the lives of everybody. They tax, borrow money, conduct elections (including national elections), establish court procedures, and administer civil and criminal law. The states authorize and regulate banking, charter corporations, and exercise wide powers relating to health standards, safety, and morals.

They operate and support public schools, colleges, universities, and specialized programs of education. They run most of our prisons, parole and probation boards, and training centers for juvenile offenders; build highways and hospitals; and set the ground rules for local government.

And that is not the full picture. As one author has put it:

They require and issue our birth certificates and our burial permits; and between the alpha and omega of our mortal existence they protect our rights in various other ways. If we hunt, fish, drive a car, marry, teach, practice law or medicine, or enter into a wide variety of other professions or callings, we must have a state license. We buy, sell, lease, rent, and inherit property under state law. In short, to the extent that our activities depend upon or are controlled by government, the responsible government is usually a state or local one.[1]

The states as the laboratories of democracy have marked

up a record of positive contributions to the progress of America. Supreme Court Justice Louis D. Brandeis wrote:

It is one of the happy incidents of the federal system that a single courageous state may, if its citizens choose, serve as a laboratory and try novel social and economic experiments without risk to the rest of the country.[2]

And as Brooke Graves has added: "An experiment does not have to be successful in order to be useful. The bank-deposit guarantee laws are a case in point. Eleven states adopted legislation of this type, but none of them were regarded as notably successful." For various reasons all of them were repealed. "Yet the very weaknesses revealed by a study of this experience enabled the Federal Government to establish guidelines and devise the pattern for a system that has operated successfully since 1933." [3]

The states have often filled the role of the experimenter and the innovator, and they continue to do so. The era of Woodrow Wilson in New Jersey, Theodore Roosevelt in New York, and Robert La Follette in Wisconsin is well known for innovative state action. Not only was it a time of new things in state government, but in the absence of activity by the national government, the states were leading the way in the regulation of economic interests, in labor reforms, in food and health laws, and in civil-rights legislation.

The "Wisconsin Idea" was not simply a theory, but a practical and coherent program actually in effect between 1900 and 1914.

To insure and enlarge the functions of representative government, the progressives of Wisconsin . . . put into operation a direct primary, an initiative and referendum, a corrupt-practices act, a law governing campaign expenditures, a civil service law, and an anti-lobbying law. . . . The State set up transportation, industrial, and public utility commissions to fix rates and guarantee services . . . a state income tax, an inheritance tax, regulatory life insurance and banking laws, an act to assist co-operatives, an unfair-trade-practices act, new weights and measures regulations, and laws governing stock and bucket-shop operations. . . . It had child- and female-labor laws, industrial safety laws, public health and pure food laws, a workmen's compensation act, a conservation law . . . education and extension work. The "Wisconsin Idea" was a progressive experiment in democracy that worked.[4]

As for Woodrow Wilson's tenure in New Jersey, Duane Lockard describes his inaugural message as one which

made those of his predecessors look like bedtime stories: he announced his intention of pursuing a broad program of reforms: in corporations, labor laws, public utilities, primary elections and the referendum, ballot reform, even concerning high food prices . . . he got bills drafted for submission and proceeded to do everything he could think of to move them along.[5]

Historian Arthur Link says, "Although Wilson was not the first American governor to recognize the vast potentialities inherent in the executive's position as a party leader, no governor in our history has ever made better use of his political opportunities and potentialities. . . ."[6]

And in New York State, Theodore Roosevelt relates the following achievements during his governorship at the turn of the century:

I secured the re-enactment of the civil service law . . . a mass of labor legislation . . . a tenement-house commission . . . [laws to] improve sweat-shop labor, to make the eight-hour and prevailing rate of wages law effective, . . . enforcement of the act relating to the hours of railway-workers, to compel railways to equip freight-trains with air-brakes, to regulate the working hours of women and protect both women and children from dangerous machinery . . . to provide seats for the use of waitresses . . . to reduce the hours of labor for drugstore clerks. . . . I tried hard but failed to secure an employers' liability law. . . . I was able to do a great deal for forest preservation and the protection of our wild life. All that later I strove for in the nation in connection with conservation was foreshadowed by what I strove to obtain for New York State when I was Governor.[7]

In California, Hiram Johnson sought the governorship on the slogan, "Kick the corporations out of politics." To achieve his objectives he organized his own party, got his own legislators elected, and then put through the necessary legislation, which was mainly aimed at the railroads.[8]

Individual states were operating at the perimeter, leading the nation, ahead of the citizens and pointing the way against a reluctant judiciary. This was a time when the U.S. Supreme Court was overruling much state action, especially in wage and hours statutes, price and rate regulation, progressive taxes, and even certain public expenditures—all areas the Court felt beyond the states' power to regulate.

All through the 1920s, the active governments were state governments. While Harding, Coolidge, and Hoover were presiding over a languid national government, the administrations of Governors Alfred E. Smith and Franklin D. Roosevelt in New York helped get the homework ready for the New Deal. In addition, Smith's four terms were crowned with complete reorganization of the state governmental structure.

State initiative is not all history. The states have continued to pioneer in many ways. The state of California has probed the intriguing possibilities of using space-age techniques to solve community problems. Four aerospace firms were asked to look into the problems of transportation, waste disposal, crime and correction, and information collection and control. Governor Edmund G. Brown asked:

Can the same systems development skills that put John Glenn into orbit be used to cut the time a commuter must spend between home and the office? Can the kind of "new dimension" thinking that found a way to get a moon probe off the launching pad also find a way to get able-bodied men off the welfare rolls? [9]

I am not sure these preliminary experiments have been very productive so far, but that is not the point. They indicate a creative direction toward a greater use in government of the techniques of our new technology.

New York State has begun a most far-reaching assault on water pollution. The need was dramatically illustrated by the recent droughts in the Northeast, when water rationing was required in New York City even though 11 billion gallons of water, grossly polluted, flow by the city daily. Some funds for pollution control are going to be made available from the national government over the next several years. New York could have waited, but Governor Nelson Rockefeller did not choose to wait. He felt the state should show its determination to get on with its urgent responsibility; to start a clean-up campaign when it was needed, and not at some future date when outside funds will be available. As a result the voters approved, by a four-to-one margin, the second largest state bond issue in history, for $1.6 billion. Here the state is leading and stimulating activity, although all three levels of government are involved.

In Kentucky, by almost every measure a Southern state, Governor Bert T. Combs, in an act of singular political courage, assured Negroes access to places of public accommodation by executive order in 1963. He based his order on the state's inherent police power to license and regulate businesses within the state, including restaurants, hotels, and motels.

In 1966, a civil-rights bill proposed by Governor Edward T. Breathitt, broader in scope than the federal act of 1964, was passed by the Kentucky legislature. The employment section of the bill brought 90 per cent of the Kentucky labor force under the law, compared to 60 per cent that will be covered by the federal law when it reaches its most extensive coverage in July, 1968. The bill passed in the Kentucky House of Representatives by a vote of 76 to 12, and in the Senate by 36 to 1. In signing the bill into law, Governor Breathitt said it "was a moral commitment kept after a hundred years of hope deferred—a promissory note long overdue." It was also a demonstration of what a state can do in providing leadership to the nation, even going well beyond the national policy.

In corrections and prisoner rehabilitation, states have long broken new ground in attempts to rehabilitate rather than merely punish the prisoner. This attitude is reflected by the comment made by the chief administrator of one of our largest state's corrections system: "We have to aim at correction rather than punishment of the prisoner. Nearly all of them return to society; so we have to prepare them for this. And we really must follow them right into the community to make sure they are adjusting and fitting back in." The purpose is to use what energy and imagination are necessary to keep a prisoner from ever coming back to prison. As long ago as 1913 a state established the first work-release program. Selected inmates were allowed to leave prison during the day to work in private employment. It took some time for the idea to prove its worth and to catch on in other states, but now at least half of the states are developing similar programs in which the prisoner receives his pay from his private employer, and in turn pays the prison for his room and board, turning the remainder over for family support or to be held until he is released. The Federal Bureau of Prisons began such a program under the Federal Rehabilitation Act of 1965.[10] This is an excellent example of the states as laboratories to test an innovative idea in a sensitive area and develop it into enlightened practice. Prison reform is continuing in the states. Innovations such as community centers and special personnel training programs, for example, are again illustrative of the states' capacity for experimental and creative reform.

The Federal Highway Safety Program has captured many

headlines in the last few months. Every recommendation now carried forward by national action has come from the laboratories of the states, and the experience they have gained over many years of making our highways safer. For example, at the beginning of 1967, thirty-two states now authorize, and in some cases require, driver education in high schools; eighteen states have developed "implied consent" laws under which a driver suspected of driving under the influence of alcohol is deemed to have consented in advance to a chemical blood test by virtue of exercising his driving privilege; thirty-three states have established either total or spot safety inspection of motor vehicles; forty-four states belong to a Vehicle Equipment Safety Compact [11] which promotes uniformity in state laws relating to motor-vehicle equipment; and twenty-one states have joined an interstate compact for the exchange of information on violations of traffic laws by nonresident motorists.[12] Numerous other individual state programs work toward safer highways. The new Federal Highway Safety Act not only is beholden to the states for its program, but builds is provisions upon their experience.

The mental-health programs in our country have been shaped and advanced by state action. The states have, by individual and cooperative effort, developed the new attitudes about mental health and the improved care and treatment for mental illnesses. Kentucky has innovated in providing trained personnel for mental-health services; New York recently adopted progressive regulations to liberalize admission provisions and enhance the protection of patients; Illinois has developed a system of regional state-hospital clinics based on the community-center concept; and Maryland and Massachusetts reorganized their mental-health efforts in 1966 toward regional, community-based programs and facilities.[13] "States generally have endeavored to substitute active treatment for custodial care, and to develop new means of helping the mentally afflicted. The most intensive efforts probably have gone into expanding various services in the community, and community participation has been enhanced." [14] Thirty-three states had joined the Interstate Compact on Mental Health by January 1, 1967.[15] Among other things, it sets up reciprocal treatment without regard to legal residence. The states have provided the impetus for progress as the leading partners in the field of mental health.

Any list of state achievements must include education many times and in many forms. Over the years the states have carried a major portion of the support for education. State leadership sounded the call for universal education. The states and their subdivisions expanded our system from the one-room schoolhouse to the consolidated high school. The states invented community colleges. The states and their instrumentalities found new ways to reach the retarded on one hand and the talented on the other; the states improved and extended the textbook, pioneered in the use of teaching aids and instructional film and television, and experimented with programmed instruction and almost every other method and procedure of teaching. In state after state the schools were revived in the 1930s by state aid, and continue to receive major support.

That we have lagged too long in solving our state problems is perhaps true. I do not know. Maybe we should or can move no faster than we are able to learn. But to suggest that the states have failed to spend their share of the money for major basic programs is clearly not true.

This can be illustrated by the most recent figures on two major areas of expenditures, education and highways. In primary and secondary education, the estimated 1966–1967 federal share of the total costs was less than 10 per cent, while the state share ranges from 5.4 per cent in Nebraska to 76.8 per cent in Delaware. The average state expenditure for 1966–1967 was estimated at 39.9 per cent.[16] In highway construction and maintenance, the 1965 federal share was slightly less than one-third of the total costs while the states were providing well over one-half the total costs.[17] It may surprise some people to discover that the states are doing more than the national government in these areas. But they always have and this is as it should be. The states can get more for the tax dollar, and have long accepted the important responsibility of providing these basic services.

The highway expenditures might be questioned by some who have had the impression that highways are built mostly with federal dollars. This impression may be, in part, the result of effective public relations. Most states take it for granted that the taxpayers, seeing grading and paving machines and new roads, assume the state gasoline tax is at work. But the federal government doesn't risk such assumptions. For every road built or improved, the state or the contractor must erect a sign proclaiming "Your Highway Taxes at Work" in eight-inch block letters, with the amounts of the funds from each government, and other information as required by Act of Congress (Section 114[a], Title 23) and spelled out by almost ten pages of guidelines. It is a small matter, but worth noting, that the signs applauding the work must be 6 feet by 13 feet when the federal funds are 90 per cent, in the case of the interstate system, but only 4 feet by 8 feet when the federal funds are 50 per cent of the costs. The advertising called "public relations" is a wonderful invention. All state schools must comply with the sign requirements, and even a little church college has to put the congregations in the back pews and post a red, white, and blue sign if it receives federal money under the Higher Education Facilities Act.

Maybe the greatest failing of the states over the years has been that they have not spent enough on public relations. This may be the way to success and public acknowledgment. It is estimated that there are about as many employees with public-relations assignments in the federal government as the total of elected state officials in the nation.[18]

The states, contrary to the oft-advanced assertion that they are by-passed in the federal system because they are unwilling to pay their fair share, are not remiss in spending funds for basic governmental services. The problems and the need for national funds are not reflected in comparative figures because the quality of public service cannot be measured by the amount of money expended. This must be judged in other ways, but I am certain that quality has gone up as federal contributions increased.

The states, most of them underfinanced—some because of an unwillingness of the people to accept state taxes, some because of timid leadership, many because of lack of economic resources—have struggled, sometimes valiantly and with sacrifice, to keep the train of government moving. That at times it only chugged along can be explained by all the defects this book documents, but even when only chugging, the rate of advance was greater by far than any other government known to man's history. For the most part the states didn't have the money to improve the train service. They needed the money for new boilers, air-conditioned sleepers, self-loading freight cars. The people were demanding more streamlined service.

The money for the extras came from the national funds. In government services the national funds provide extra teachers, the projectors and other equipment, the films and slides, the new library books in the schools; the free money for planning in the cities; the new medical equipment of the university; the civil-defense radios. The new and bright additions to old, regular programs all came because there was new federal grant money made available. This is the glamour money, all federal in appearances. It is needed, it has improved the quality, and that is why it was appreciated. It is proper to remember, however, for all the advantages brought by the extras, the train was put on the track in the first place by the states, and continues to be moved by state fuel and engineers.

The quality achieved by the states' contributions varies from activity to activity. In at least one activity, it is undisputed that over the years the money from the states has achieved excellence. That is public higher education.

Except for Howard and a few municipal colleges, the state governments almost monopolize the public provision of higher education. . . . A key element of the American dream, advancement and success by means of education and technical training, has always been associated with state governments. The state university is one institution in which all citizens of the state . . . have a direct or potential interest.[19]

The nation has become strong through the support the states have given public higher education. The national government could develop the atomic bomb, our space sciences, and the World War II technology only because of our state systems of higher education. Much of our pre-eminence as a social and governmental system has come from our unrivaled state-based university and college system. Even the land-grant college, initially established under the impetus of federal land grants provided by the Morrill Act of 1863, has been mainly supported by state appropriations through the years, with only minimal funds from the national government. The states made higher education what it is, from the first state universities in North Carolina and Georgia to the most recent community college in Oregon. The university capacity of America couldn't have been put together in a crash program. It has grown over many years by state nurture.

Finally, states represent communities of people loyal to their state. Most have been educated in their state's school system, and live in the state's cultural and political environment. They take pride in being Texans, North Carolinians, Vermonters, or Oregonians, especially in the fall when the state university's football team is in gear. There are cynics who question this sense of community in an age when the U.S. Census Bureau indicates that "each year one in every five Americans moves." Yet behind that broad figure of moving Americans lies the reality that only three out of every one hundred Americans actually changed their state of residence between March, 1959, and March, 1960, and even this figure is inflated by the movement of college students, the military, and those who "move from St. Louis, Missouri, to East St. Louis, Illinois, or from the Bronx, New York, to Teaneck, New Jersey." And this percentage was less than the movement of a century earlier.[20]

While there is disagreement as to the strength of this notion of community, its impact on our governmental structure is summed up by York Willbern:

There is, to be sure, a degree of unity or sense of community which is attached to our states as units of history and tradition and, so important that it cannot be discounted, by the very fact of political organization. These attachments are sufficiently strong that any suggestion for changing state boundaries or reshuffling the deck at this level is completely unrealistic politically.[21]

The states are here to stay. The genuine question, the one we can do something about, the one worth our attention, is how we might shape the states' actions, not their boundaries, for the most effective response to their citizens' needs.

Governor Carl E. Sanders (Georgia, 1963–67), in a letter acknowledging we have failed "to assume many responsibilities that rightfully should be dealt with on a state level," had this to add: "I personally believe that the states today still represent the most important and effective unit in our entire system of government, and that the roles which they play can become more important—and not less important—as many fear."[22]

There is a noticeable feeling throughout the states that the time has come for them to assert leadership boldly. This is a new spirit, calling ever better men and women to service in state government and politics.

Those who believe in the federal system must of necessity believe in improved state governments. In the history and the present performance of states there is much to reinforce this belief, and to encourage those who would undertake the strengthening of state structures. While it is easy and shallow simply to rail at increasing centralization of the national government, it is equally superficial to lampoon the states as an inadequate institution of American government because of the imperfections or activities of individual states.

There are those who are fond of playing a game which might be entitled, "But Look at Alabama!" Today it is Alabama, yesterday it was a different state, and tomorrow it will be yet another. This is their rebuttal to every suggestion that the states should be built up, reinforced, reformed, given added responsibilities, and developed as a more important division of the American federal system. But this is no answer at all. This is a political and partisan response, an expression of the disputant's opinion about a particular state, and there is no purpose to be served by arguing the merits of his opinion. It would be easy to counter his answer by saying, "But look at Hughes of New Jersey, Chafee of Rhode Island, Mc-Keithan of Louisiana, Kerner of Illinois, Hughes of Iowa, Hoff of Vermont, Connally of Texas, Rockefeller of New York, McNair of South Carolina, and many others." But this is no answer either. Personalities are not the relevant argument. Surely there are governors who by either action or inaction weaken the image of state government generally. But surely no one would suggest seriously today, as Alexander Hamilton did in 1787, that in order to get the "right kind" of governors, they should be selected by Congress or appointed by the President. The people of the states will continue to elect their governors, and if the people make mistakes, democracy must endure the mistakes. To use these mistakes as arguments to weaken the federal system by weakening the states is no more justified than arguing that the national government is inefficient because the Post Office Department cannot get out of the red. Mistakes by the people, if they are mistakes, cannot be fuel to forge the reshaping of the structure of our federal government. There are other ways of redress, called into use on many occasions in our history. The U.S. Constitution guarantees "to every State in this Union a Republican form of Government." If abuses require additional laws to protect the republican form, then there is evidence aplenty that our system can produce the necessary laws. If the frailties of man result in imperfect administration of government, as they assuredly will from time to time, the answer is not to abolish or weaken our institutions of popular control of politics.

The states have served the people well. There is a long list of solid and reassuring achievement in every state to bear out this conclusion. They have the capacity to serve even better if we will quit fussing and start thinking, quit fumbling and start working, and make the changes which will enable the states to fulfill their role effectively as a part of our federal structure.

1. Claudius O. Johnson and Associates, *American State and Local Government*, (New York: Thomas Y. Crowell Company, 1965), p. 2.
2. Dissenting opinion in *New State Ice Co. v. Liebmann*, 285 U.S. 262, p. 311, (1932).
3. W. Brooke Graves, "Creative Federalism's Challenge to the States," unpublished paper prepared for The Committee on Economic Development, July 5, 1966, p. 7.
4. Russel B. Nye, *Midwestern Progressive Politics*, (East Lansing: Michigan State University Press, 1959), pp. 201–202.
5. Duane Lockard, *The New Jersey Governor; A Study in Political Power*, (Princeton, New Jersey: D. Van Nostrand Company, Inc., 1964), pp. 108–109.
6. Arthur S. Link, *Wilson, The Road to the White House*, (Princeton, New Jersey: Princeton University Press, 1947), p. 249.
7. Wayne Andrews (ed.), *The Autobiography of Theodore Roosevelt*, (New York: Charles Scribner's Sons, 1958), pp. 156–157.
8. Leslie Lipson, *The American Governor from Figurehead to Leader*, (Chicago: University of Chicago Press, 1938), pp. 50–51.
9. Edmund G. Brown, "Aerospace Studies for the Problems of Men," *State Government*, Vol. XXXIX, (Winter, 1966), p. 2.
10. *The Book of the States, 1966–1967*, Vol. XVI, (Chicago: The Council of State Governments, 1966), pp. 390–391.

11. Interstate compacts are multistate arrangements between states, similar to contracts between individuals. A more thorough discussion occurs in Chapter XII.

12. *Book of the States, 1966–1967*, pp. 322–327; "Action by the Legislatures: 1966," *State Government*, XXXIX, (Autumn, 1966), pp. 277–279; and *Interstate Compacts, 1783–1966: A Compilation*, (Chicago: The Council of State Governments, 1966), pp. 71, 89–90.

13. Harold L. McPheeters, "Making the Most of Mental Health Manpower," *State Government*, XXXIX, (Spring, 1966), pp. 92–96; Hyman M. Forstenzer, "New York's New Directions in Mental Health Services," *ibid.*, Vol. XXXVII, (Autumn, 1964), pp. 235–241; Donald Brieland, Community Mental Health, The Illinois Program," *ibid.*, Vol. XXXVI, (Spring, 1963), pp. 112–117; "Action by the Legislatures: 1966," *ibid.*, Vol. XXXIX, (Autumn, 1966), pp. 276–277.

14. Ruth Turk, "State Mental Health Programs, 1964–1965," *Book of the States, 1966–1967*, p. 340.

15. *Interstate Compacts, 1783–1966: A Compilation*, p. 76.

16. Committee on Educational Finance, *What Everyone Should Know about Financing Our Schools* (Washington: National Education Association, 1966, revised 1967), pp. 49, 55.

17. U.S. Bureau of the Census, *Statistical Abstract of the United States: 1966*, 87th edition, (Washington: U.S. Government Printing Office, 1966), p. 421.

18. *The World Journal Tribune*, (New York), March 19, 1966, reported, "The government expends about $425 million a year on its public information, news, views, and self-pleadings. . . . Manning the sluice gates of this stream of self-revelation are at least 6858 federal employees occupied full or part time." We can add to this at least one for each congressional office.

There are 7599 state legislators and 758 other elected officials (including judges).

19. Samuel Huntington, in York Willbern, "States as Components in Areal Division of Powers," Arthur Maass, (ed.), *Area and Power*, (Glencoe, Illinois: The Free Press, 1959), pp. 87–88.

20. Ben J. Wattenberg with Richard M. Scammon, *This U.S.A.*, (Garden City, New York: Doubleday & Company, 1965), pp. 112–116.

21. York Willbern, *op. cit.*, p. 76.

22. Letter from Carl E. Sanders, former Governor of Georgia, January 23, 1967.

CHAPTER VIII

The Limited Reach of the National Government

I once opened a speech on a university campus by announcing my title: "The New Deal Was a Failure." The students were somewhat shocked. They had been taught that the New Deal was America's salvation. Many of them felt from their own study that the New Deal was the coming of age of a democracy, now adjusted to the needs of an intricate industrial society. The New Deal had set up the machinery to ease the problems of every citizen, rich or poor, with compassion and power. I happen to agree with the students.

The point is, or so I contended, that in fact the New Deal did not reach nearly all the people it set out to serve. With all its permanent benefits, it did not lift the burden of an inscrutable economic system from the back of the disadvantaged and uneducated citizen. Nor did it relieve from our economic system the weight of the nonproductive citizen.

In 1937 President Franklin D. Roosevelt eloquently called for action to lift up the one-third of the nation "ill-housed, ill-clad, and ill-nourished." But a quarter of a century later it was still necessary for President Johnson to ask the Congress "to help that one-fifth of all American families with income too small even to meet their basic needs." That some 20 per cent of our people are still have-nots argues not so much the failure of the dream of the New Deal as our failure to realize fully this dream in action.

President Roosevelt's first act was to revive banking. The crumbling ribs of society's sturdiest institution demanded attention. The first step was to proclaim a bank holiday. Then followed the Emergency Banking Act, and a few weeks later the abandonment of the gold standard, and in yet another few weeks the insured deposits. From this start, not many will deny, flowed immense steadying forces to shield the economy from violent business cycles and severe depressions. New Deal legislation was also directed at recovery, diminishing unemployment, improvement of working conditions, and care of the old, the afflicted, and the dependent. It sought to eliminate the social ills that held the American opportunity beyond the reach of many people. Some of these objectives are now realities in our national life; others are not yet realized.

The Agriculture Adjustment Act and subsequent legislation generally saved the farmer in the 1930s and put the commercial farmer in a profitable position for the 1950s and 1960s. But the farm programs, which have several times changed composition and complexion, if not direction, have not brought full opportunity to people whose livelihood comes from farming. Today the fruits of prosperity and the comforts of life still hang far too high for the sharecropper, the migrant worker, the family farmer with a family larger than his acreage, and the displaced worker. The farmer's return on his investment of capital, time, and toil is far less than that enjoyed by business. Nonproductive residents, marginal workers, and undercompensated farmers remain a drag on our economy. Poverty in farm areas continues to smother the spirit of the rural people.

The number of substandard, and even uninhabitable, rural houses constitutes a nationwide disgrace, if not scandal. Reliable figures list 3,614,381 such dwellings, some 20.5 per cent of our rural houses, as substandard. And another 8 per cent are deteriorating.[1] There is no measure of how many shacks are totally unfit for children.

The flow of country people to the cities is symptomatic of numerous rural ills. That the rush is to an even harsher life is beside the point. They leave a place where they see no opportunity for a place where they dream they will find it. Almost always the dream is a delusion, and they discover they did not advance on new and bright horizons. Rather, they retreated into the cloudy and dreary nightfall. They traded nothing for less than nothing.

"The move from American farms over the last twenty years (1940–1960)," Ben Wattenberg pointed out, "has been one of the greatest single migrations in the history of the world . . . more farm people left farms than remained. . . ."[2]

When the policies of agricultural adjustment were being shaped in the 1930s there was a conflict for a while between the plight of the tenant and the support of the landlord. The circumstances favored the landowner. The immediate need was to make farming profitable, and the dirt farmer could wait. To a large extent he is still waiting. The numerous U.S. Department of Agriculture agencies, bureaus, committees, and boards, from their vested positions, have run the machinery of the governmental involvement in agriculture. That involvement has been tremendous. It has absorbed attention and energies of all levels of government. It has drawn matching money from the county commissioners (or other local authority) who may have held a veto in theory, but in reality have had little choice except to provide money and office space as their share in the problem solving. In fact, the agricultural programs created a new battery of local governments with no lines of authority or decision to elected local government.

The states have played no substantial role in the stabilization of the agricultural economy. True, they have their own departments of agriculture, but most of their functions relate to keeping sawdust out of chicken feed and sand out of fertilizer, or otherwise protecting the consumer. The states, for some matching contribution as the admission charge, were assigned good seats in the bleachers from which they could only observe the game of improving the lot of rural America. There was, of course, the Extension Service. But for all these years the land-grant college, the Extension Service, and the USDA empire have never been more than politely and magnanimously unresponsive to the influence of state government.

Little fault can be found with what was done through the federal programs. Secretary of Agriculture Orville L. Freeman said, "Since its founding, and until very recently, the Department has been almost exclusively concerned with agriculture—keeping its records, researching its problems, conserving its soil, and educating its constituency in scientific farming." [3] Sadly, until very recently, this has been true.

Much fault can be found with what was not done. Maybe rural poverty, dwindling towns and villages, and the migration to the cities were not concerns of government. But the administrators of the massive agriculture programs were not making a conscious decision to leave them alone. They were just left alone.

The criticism is that the vast national mechanism for agriculture sealed itself off from new ideas and local innovations. It placed no premium on looking for new problems, let alone testing new or experimental solutions. Indeed it thwarted other actions, and, it could be argued, placed some kind of unspoken premium on not looking for new problems. The mechanism occupied the field. Agriculture was its domain, and national direction, once set, became direction across the nation. Elected government, state and local, had no way to change, or deflect, or broaden, or guide the national direction. The argument is against inflexible finality in action, against the centralization of idea and program. The creative addition at the bottom of the system was discouraged or prohibited. There was a role for the states, but they were never allowed to play it. The lesson born out of our only partially successful experiences is that this is not the way we should shape government programs needed today.

Poverty in the early 1930s was not confined to the rural areas. Nor is it today. The most hopeless poverty was in the cities, where it still is. The soup lines demanded quick action. The states did not have enough money and many cities were flat broke. The national government in 1933 was compelled to assume the cost of public relief.

After such emergency measures as the WPA, the NIRA, the PWA, and the CCC, Congress enacted permanent social security legislation. Part of this act set up the payment of benefits to old people in a totally national program, presently administered by the Social Security Administration. Another part, Title II, was the beginning of the public welfare program, now the Welfare Administration in the Department of Health, Education, and Welfare. Originally it provided for payments to people too old to participate in and benefit from social security.

This program was established with the idea of involving the states. First, welfare had been a state and local responsibility. Second, Secretary Frances Perkins, who led in the development of the welfare programs, brought a state point of view from her previous job as Industrial Commissioner of the state of New York.

But what started out in a spirit of cooperative effort among local, state, and national governments was soon pinned down by a heavy, regulation-ridden monolith which has for years operated beyond effective control by national, state, or local government. The controls applied to those who needed help and guidance. Unemployed fathers had to abandon, or pretend to abandon, their families before they could get aid for their children. No realistic ways were developed to help welfare recipients become self-supporting.

Although these programs were established to be "income replacement" programs, we now find a new group of poor on our hands—the welfare-program poor. These people, receiving aid under one of the five programs originally set up in 1935, find the income provided by the government too small to live on. But to attempt a job is to lose the payments, and there is no device for transition from job to job until the recipient earns enough to jettison the welfare payments. Of this situation Leon Keyserling said:

. . . after three decades, this array [of social insurance and welfare payments] has failed. As of late 1966 among those aged 65 and over receiving [Social Security] benefits, between two-fifths and three-fifths lived in poverty, taking into account their income from all sources. . . . Among those aged 65 and over who receive Old Age Assistance but do not receive [Social Security] benefits, about nine out of ten live in poverty.[4]

In these welfare programs the states were given the role of administrator. This means that each state had to draw up a plan of action. But the "plans" are not plans as the word is popularly used; they are really budgets which list numbers of recipients, categories of aid, and costs of the program. The plans detailed no goal other than getting the proper amount of aid to the proper people. A state or local government was not expected to suggest that funds be used to carry out, for instance, an experimental program in employment or in aid to dependent children of unemployed fathers. Flexibility was considered to be inefficiency. Deviation was an ugly word. Locally this policy was incarnated in a harried social worker (selected, it is true, on the basis of higher and higher professional standards), with a caseload three times too large, and obliged to follow standardized procedures and report them on standard forms. The system itself had little place for sympathy, and still less for the innovative approaches the problems demanded. The only saving grace of the welfare program was the sympathetic concern of the individual welfare department employee as a human being.

The problem of able-bodied citizens out of work has long been one of society's problems. Since New Deal days our efforts furnish a unique example of federal-state relations.[5] While some states had systems of public employment offices before World War I, it was in 1932 that Wisconsin, under Governor Philip F. La Follette, enacted the first unemployment compensation plan, with each company working out its own unemployment reserves. In the same year Ohio proposed that contributions be pooled in a single fund—with contributions from both employee and employer. Others felt that since no employee or employer was responsible for most unemployment, government should contribute, as in Britain. Until 1933 the responsibility for employment services was clearly that of the states, and there was no national government activity. In 1933 the Wagner-Peyser Act provided for a 50-50 federal matching grant for administration of state programs with certain minimal standards (e.g., merit systems for state personnel). Under this program "the states enjoyed a very high degree of independence" and the total state and federal funds involved were relatively small.[6] However, only eight states adopted a program under this act.

The Social Security Act of 1935 changed the entire structure of the program. No federal system of compensation was established, but the Act did force the other forty states to establish an unemployment compensation system of their own in order to recapture nine-tenths of a payroll tax levied by the national government. Thus, in addition to administrative funds, programmatic funds were nationally based. The programs became nearly 100 per cent federally financed while state-administered.

The administrative grants were made to the states under criteria which stressed the "proper and efficient" administration of the program, with the U.S. Employment Service officials serving as judges of the states' efforts. Soon Federal directives and guidelines began to exercise greater control over the budgets which governed the expenditures by the states. Federal officials acted as guideline setters and budget reviewers while the state officials were reduced to being administrators. In this way, the states lost their leeway for action.

Then the action to "federalize" all state employment services during World War II and the later return to the federal-state relationship further muddled the image as being little more than an administrative arm of a national program. Edison Bowers and William Papier set the problem of the states' role succinctly:

We have been gradually approaching a complete federal system by the back door—a system in which the state legislatures and the state administrators relinquish their rights and responsibilities in return for administrative funds. Adoption by Congress of minimum benefit standards, enforceable by federal financial controls, would doubtless sound the death knell for current remnants of state administration.[7]

There is no evidence here that most states would have done a better job. Nearly all of them became involved only because of national legislation. Probably the industrial special interests in most of these states had adequate influence to hold back state legislation. The national push was necessary.

The record, however, is one of only partial success. The

unemployment compensations protected purchasing power and cushioned against downward business cycles. Employment figures have been rising, but credit for this can hardly go to the employment security commissions. The various employment services promoted the employment of the handicapped with imagination; they developed public announcements of information about available jobs. They provided a counseling service, matching available men with available jobs.

They left untouched a number of other needs. They didn't consider it their problem to identify the unemployable, guiding them to health and educational services which would make them employable. It wasn't "proper and efficient" administration to help the ignorant and uneducated get prepared for jobs. They developed no way of recruiting the unemployed who by their very lack of qualifications would never come near the brick and glass offices of the employment services. The employment services were not looking for new problems. To do so would run counter to established procedures. There was no reward for finding new solutions.

State government had no administrative key with which to switch on new and different approaches. Reaching the newly discovered and constantly emerging needs of people without jobs or with inadequate jobs required special state projects, private foundation funds, a national anti-poverty war, and some restructuring of federal government.

I do not insist that the states alone and unencouraged would have done better than the national government. They would not have, except a few. The answer is a different kind of intergovernmental relationship—one that provides the urge, sets the minimums, but doesn't dominate with iron-handed direction—one that leaves open the right of the state to move in new directions, make some mistakes, seek other problems, try out various solutions.

In 1917, the Smith-Hughes Act began federal grant-in-aid support for vocational education "to fit persons for useful employment." The program called for training in agriculture, trades and industry, and home economics, but as it developed it became, in keeping with the needs of the day, heavily oriented toward agriculture. Local and state matching funds followed these grants and set the tone for vocational education long after agriculture had ceased to be the most pressing need in most parts of the nation. In 1963, Congress opened up the entire vocational education program. Now the states and local school districts have freedom to develop vocational training according to their own needs, rather than having just a choice of adding or not adding matching money for a set program. The training in agriculture was good and continues usefully in some schools; but times had changed and there was no local way to widen the program with the changing times. Major action by Congress was required to put vocational education back on course almost a generation late.

The nation's housing problem has been attacked by an unusual group of programs. The policy behind government housing laws is complex and their targets are varied. One basic purpose is to keep the major industry of home building growing and a goodly section of our labor force busy. Housing policy was to be one of the devices to maintain full employment and to battle recessions—and, as we have seen recently, to control inflation. Second, the programs aid the individual home buyer, the builder, the land developer, or the city renewer, but not all at once. Some federal assistance goes to local government, and some to the individual citizen. There is little or no coordination among the programs.

The states never had much part in the federal housing program; they only prescribed codes and established other regulations, and some have assumed other responsibilities for housing. Local governments have been concerned with zoning, building inspection, and related activities, including public housing and urban redevelopment, but have not had much influence on execution of the federal programs. Their participation is often more apparent than real.

The programs in housing lack focus and clear purpose. The federal government, and in some cases the states and local governments, is putting funds into the housing market, building and rebuilding, structuring and restructuring communities—all without really having a clear battle plan. We do not know which directions are the best, so we go in all directions.

Programs run into each other and guidelines contradict guidelines. Individual homes can receive improvement loans, but neighborhoods cannot. In fact, a neighborhood must become almost fully deteriorated (a slum) before it can be improved. Subdivisions can be approved and developed if they are in open countryside. But if they are near slums or if slums are encroaching on the area, the homes cannot be insured even though a new subdivision might improve the value of the land and lead to the removal of the slums. The answer to an application is no; the slums might endanger the value of the homes. Besides, slum clearance is not the responsibility of the agency insuring home loans.

More states should be involved directly in housing problems. Why not involve them and call upon them for a positive contribution? Perhaps the states are in the best position to support, coordinate, and lead in zoning, planning land use, developing low-cost housing, preventing slums, and working toward adequate housing. This might be the best way to start a battle plan. Most housing problems are beyond the financial resources of any city. They are too much for the too many national programs, even though the programs have been gathered under the Department of Housing and Urban Development. Here is an opportunity for this department to try out the idea of creative federalism: to call the states into action, state by state, for originating and coordinating.

The examples discussed here are illustrative. There are better stories and worse stories of our governmental system, but these typical ones may help define our tasks. The many programs have spawned brigades of specialists for each program. There are vocational specialists, housing specialists of several varieties, social-work specialists, rehabilitation specialists, employment specialists, and the ubiquitous bureaucrats who control these programs. The communication is carried on up and down the line. There is little communication between line programs. A county welfare agent talks easily and often to welfare officials in his state capital and in Washington, but rarely to his county health agent. Administrators and their departments continue to look at problems only through the lenses of their directives, in their own limited terms. Yet many problems today span the responsibilities of government.

Government is not, in these major programs at least, like a rail fence, with three rails one above the other, one for the national, one for the state, one for the cities and local governments. It is more like a picket fence. The lines of authority, the concerns and interests, the flow of the money, and the direction of programs run straight down like a number of pickets stuck into the ground. There is, as in a picket fence, a connecting cross slat, but that does little to support anything. In this metaphor it stands for the governments. It holds the pickets in line; it does not bring them together. The picket-like programs are not connected at the bottom. Maybe we need to find some way to connect them there, some close-to-the-ground exchange for all that our agencies do.

For that matter, I see no evidence that they are even coordinated. The welfare office sees poverty as a problem of welfare, the office of education as a problem of education, the health officials as a matter of public health. Each has its programs, its guidelines and criteria—and never the slew shall meet.

The impact that this specialization and consequent fragmentation of effort has had on our people can be illustrated by a single case. In a medium-sized Southern city there is a family with insurmountable and unbelievable problems. The North Carolina Fund found that in the last two years this family has been "worked on" by forty-six separate governmental and interested public and private agencies. Each agency has its own interests, its own rules, regulations, and criteria, often to the exclusion of all others. Each is attacking its segment of the problem separately. In listening to this case history, which continues as you read this, I got a feeling of incredulity—can this be a true story? Do we really have that many agencies lurking around? We do, and while even the casual observer may find it upsetting, it is even more jolting to the family being "helped."

The states may not have been very successful in the past with society's problems, but neither have the national agencies. One reason is that no easy way to join hands at the bottom has been developed. The government agencies are mono-professional, but people are multi-problemed. The agency personnel have long looked at their programs instead of looking at people in need of help, because that is how their jobs are defined. The people who present themselves for help are considered "clients" for the agency's particular service, when in reality they are problems wrapped up in many problems. It cannot be denied that the massive national programs have not reached their mark. They may have hit the target, but they missed the bull's-eye. I am well aware that several departments, under direction of several cabinet members, are attempting to change. They must, and they must in ways they haven't yet been willing to admit. The failures so far chalked up against the poverty war, for example, are the very failures our experience should have taught us to anticipate. There are still a multiplicity of effort, jealousies between departments and agencies within departments, and skillful refusal to coordinate or be coordinated.

When the planning task force for drawing up plans for the war on poverty, made up of bright young men on loan from numerous agencies and departments, was sitting around the conference table, I knew they were there to help the general plan, but I got the impression that their first purpose was to protect the interests of the chiefs who loaned them. (I can think of three exceptions.) That the Office of Economic Opportunity has emerged, in effect, as just another agency, stymied from tying together a combination of many services to meet any combination of needs an individual might possess, is evidence of how well the planners protected their own agencies. This does not indicate total failure of our combined effort to eliminate the causes of poverty in America. It does forebode, within the accuracy of a percentage point or two, that the President of the United States in 1980 will be using the words of Roosevelt and Johnson to describe the one-eighth of the population unable to share in the opportunities of an even more affluent America.

Somewhere we must find the new approach that looks at the problems whole, be they problems of people, housing, farming, or neighborhoods. Part of the solution will be found by building state governments into the programs as coordinators of the operations down where the problems exist, with freedom to seek out the new and developing variations of the problems, with authority to insist on the discard of jurisdictional squabbles, and with encouragement to strike out on innovative and promising new ventures. I believe the states, renewed by new responsibilities, provide our best extension of the limited reach from which most government programs have suffered. The states afford much promise for a Congress that would like to see its enactments reach all the way.

1. *Congress and the Nation, 1945–1964*, (Washington: Congressional Quarterly Service, 1965), p. 467.
2. Ben J. Wattenberg with Richard M. Scammon, *This U.S.A.*, (Garden City, New York: Doubleday & Company, 1965), p. 65.
3. Address by Orville L. Freeman, to the Rural Poverty Conference, Washington, D.C., January 30, 1967.
4. Leon H. Keyserling, "Guaranteed Annual Incomes," *New Republic*, (March 18, 1967), p. 23.
5. For a general history of this federal-state program as observed in the State of Minnesota see Francis E. Rourke, *Intergovernmental Relations in Employment Security*, (Minneapolis: University of Minnesota Press, 1952).
6. Paper by Edison L. Bowers and William Papier (Ohio State Advisory Council on Unemployment Compensation), "The Employment Security Elephant," presented at IAPES Conference, University of Alabama, Tuscaloosa, March 27, 1958, p. 2.
7. *Ibid.*, p. 9.

CHAPTER IX

The Mouth of the Gift Horse

The old movie *Cimarron* [1] was recalled by an Eastern governor in describing the developing federal system of grants.

"You remember the scene of the carts, covered wagons, and buggies all lined up ready to start the land rush to Oklahoma homesites. The horses are the federal grants, let's say. They get the wagons off dead center. They start things moving with fresh power. That's good.

"Suppose, before the start signal, big blinders were put on the horses so they couldn't see the other horses. Suppose the drivers have one or both hands tied, or there are six drivers each with a part of a rein. Some of the wagons have no driver, and the reins are tied to the seat or left hanging loose.

"The horses are moving the wagons, but not many of them know where they are going, or with whom. Some go in the opposite direction. Some run into canyons. Some run over each other. Not many of them will get to the homestead country.

"This is the kind of confusion and lack of direction we now have. A federalism with grants-in-aid furnishing additional push is needed . . . in any event we have it, and will continue to. Trouble is, these programs have sprung up from time to time with no sense of order, and the various little vested interests are so firmly dug in that I don't believe it is going to be possible to reorder the mess."

The use of grants-in-aid has grown with feverish rapidity, from three in 1900, to eighteen in 1936, to an uncertain number today, depending on how they are broken down for counting. The Office of Education, for example, has, by its own count, 112 different programs under 26 different statutory grants of authority.

According to the director of the U.S. Bureau of the Budget and the Legislative Reference Service of the Library of Congress, there are now 162 major programs. Senator Edmund Muskie's committee counts more than 170 separate aid programs. In an effort to be helpful, the Advisory Commission on Intergovernmental Relations has published a catalogue of the catalogues of these aids prepared by federal agencies, state governments, and various local government organizations. It runs to over nine pages single spaced.[2]

The numbers and the confusion of numbers indicate much of the trouble. Even if the arrangement were orderly, which it is not, it would be difficult to keep count. The Eighty-ninth Congress alone produced seventeen new resource development programs, seventeen new educational programs, twenty-one new health programs, fifteen new economic development programs, twelve new programs on city problems, and four for manpower training.

A Midwestern speaker of the House expressed a more salty view of grants. "The device is simple," he said. "The opulent father gives to the son to help with the various needs in the support of his family, and slips additional tidbits to the grandchildren when he thinks they are being neglected or he wants to please them. In return he holds the hand of firm discipline, of insistence that things be 'done his way' or not at all. This analogy is too likely to conjure up visions of Tennessee Williams' Big Daddy, ostentatiously passing out his largess, demanding his own narrow and selfish satisfactions in return. It is really not that flagrant, although at times it seems to be so." He was talking at the moment about the Highway Safety Act of 1967.

Through as many years as there have been cars, the national government has done little about safety on the highways of the country. Safety was left to state and local governments, with the police power of each being employed to achieve a respectable reduction in the killing rate from 18 in 1920 to 5.7 in 1964, with some states reducing the rate much lower.[3]

In spite of the reductions during this time, the rates of death, injury, and destruction of property have remained distressingly high. Automobile accidents have become the largest cause of death and injury to Americans under thirty-five. President Johnson pointed out to Congress that "the toll of Americans killed . . . [in highway accidents] since the introduction of the automobile is truly unbelievable. It is 1.5 million—more than all the combat deaths suffered in all our wars."

Those who have worked with state traffic safety efforts have known for years that there was one glaring obstacle: the unwillingness of Congress to tackle the automobile manufacturers. Governors and others, on occasions of periodic program inventories, have insisted that the design of automobiles and the advertising were aimed at speed and horsepower rather than passenger safety. Over the years, by interstate compact and other stopgap measures, the states have pounded away and got safer lights, safety glass, and some other improvements. But regulating automobile manufacture was not a duty of the states; although California requires exhaust control devices and there are other individual state legislative specifications, it is doubtful, under the restraints of the Constitution, whether any one state can regulate the manufacture of automobiles to be sold in interstate commerce. The manufacture had to be regulated nationally, and this was always a congressional duty.

The Christian Science Monitor in an article on October 22. 1965, indicated the ease with which the federal government shoves blame on the states for a problem that, because of its national character and the enormous powers of the interests involved, is clearly a result of federal neglect:

Up to now, the federal government has deferred to the states concerning public action toward highway accidents and injuries. The auto industry would like this jurisdictional situation to remain unchanged . . . The fifty states have been lenient in passing vehicle safety legislation. The Automobile Manufacturers Association has repeatedly praised its cooperative relationship with state motor vehicle administrators, who have strong influence on what passes the legislatures in the vehicle area.

Congress avoided an unpleasant confrontation with the powerful automobile industry until public opinion in 1966 demanded it. Then with a burst of arrogance worthy of Big Daddy, the Congress moved as if the states had been the neglectful ones all along. Dr. Eric Berne in *Games People Play* would describe it as "If it weren't for you." [4] As if to divert attention from the fact that they had been the neglectful part of the government, Congress struck out at the states, threatening to withhold a percentage of highway funds unless the states took immediate and prescribed actions to promote traffic safety. The irony and injustice of such attitudes (aside from the fact that the highway funds to be withheld are a grant-in-aid only indirectly related to promoting highway safety) can be seen more clearly when it is remembered that at the same time the government was insisting that the states adopt rigid traffic safety standards, it was caving in to the auto industry on safety design of cars. This national program has much good in it, although it is late in coming. The point is that the methods and attitudes detract from the cooperative good the act was intended to achieve. The attempt to establish a nationwide criterion as the one and only path to safety slows initiative to discover proper solutions for perhaps a decade or so. That "we are doing what we are supposed to be doing" is a comforting thought for all. But states, as they have done ever since the car became a menace, must continue looking for better and diverse ways to cut down the slaughter. The states may save their highway grants, but they will not solve their safety problems by simply going along with Congress.

Now, to be more objective, we will abandon the Tennessee Williams model of intergovernmental relations. Instead, we will turn to Morton Grodzins' more deferential and academic model. He rejected the traditional picture of federal-state-local government in America as a cake in three layers, neatly stacked on one another and neatly identifiable. Rather, he pictured intergovernmental relations as more like the rainbow or marble cake, with the colors blending and running down through the cake "in vertical and diagonal strands and unexpected whirls." [5] This is an apt image of our grant-in-aid government. Grants, support, and administration flow from all three traditional levels of government, intermingling in a way that makes it difficult to distinguish exactly where one rules, or the other concedes, or they all cooperate. This relationship has developed because the citizen has called on, perhaps deliberately and perhaps randomly, all three levels of his government.

The evidence is clear that grants-in-aid from the national government have brought about improvement in many activities of government. Grants have drawn local money and local interest into endeavors believed by Congress to be in the national interest. They have added national money to struggling state and local programs. They have put emphasis on the needs of the people requiring, in the opinion of Congress, added emphasis.

That Congress yields to the pleas of so many interests, handing out grants in such a way that they can't be counted, much less fully comprehended, raises some serious doubts. Certainly we have problems as a nation, but do we have quite as many problems rating top priority as we have grants? We are in danger of having so many spotlights that we cannot see the daylight.

Two questions were asked us constantly across the country as we talked with many officials. Why need federal grants be administered so arbitrarily, as if all wisdom were concentrated along the lower reaches of the Potomac? Why are the effort, interest, and rightful participation of the national government so fragmented, obscured, and haphazard as to give birth to an entirely new, highly specialized profession—consultant to state and local governments on national grant-in-aid programs? These questions shed much light on why "the best-selling volume in the United States today is a pristine Congressional committee print entitled *Catalog of Federal Aids to State and Local Governments.*⁶

The grants seem to redistribute the wealth of the nation, to some degree, into areas which need it most. Some rich states bemoan the fact that their people are helping foot the bill in poorer states. The North Dakota tax commissioner thinks that it is merely another demonstration of our community of interests: "In North Dakota, over half of all state and local funds go for education and yet we have a very high out-migration of college graduates. Our best earning potential ends up paying income taxes in other states. We have no way to recover any benefit from our high investment in education other than through a federal grant system."⁷

There is other reassurance for the wealthier states, if they need it. The evidence is that federal expenditures help the rich states get richer to a greater degree than they assist the poorer states by redistribution.

The greatest impact of federal spending within the United States comes not from transfers of payments but from defense-related expenditures and direct payments to private individuals. . . . Defense contracts represent the great bulk of the direct federal expenditures within the states. In fiscal 1962 alone, new contracts

... were ... approximately four times the total amount distributed through federal grants in that same year.[8]

It cannot be denied that the quality of governmental operation has been raised by the required standards of the grants-in-aid. The question, however, remains whether the acknowledged benefits of these hundreds of programs necessarily prove that giving a multitude of grants is the best way to achieve the most effective results in our intergovernmental relationships.

While a trivial matter, one example indicates the difficulty of keeping too many strings tied to the center nail, of seeking too much uniformity, or setting one pattern for all of the diverse nation. The state of Wyoming had a slight hassle with the U.S. Bureau of Public Roads over the color of paint to be used to mark the sides and center line of Wyoming highways. Wyoming had painted a solid yellow line to mark the shoulder of the road and an intermittent yellow line for the center. The Bureau of Public Roads said the lines must be standardized with the rest of the country, which meant white lines except in the no-passing stretches. After much haggling, Wyoming inevitably gave in, but with a parting comment: "Let them come out here and find one of their white lines during one of our blizzards." The highway engineers had found that in the blowing blizzards of Wyoming's winters drivers could see yellow lines, but not white ones. In this encounter they learned that yellow lines could not be seen from Washington.

More serious consequences grow out of the inability of Washington to see the refinements, differences, and special needs of each area, region, section, and locality of our vast country. One state official said succinctly: "The federal government is going to have to realize that everybody in the country doesn't live in Washington, and that every problem can't be defined in terms of Washington or Montgomery County, Maryland."

In a booklet issued in November, 1966, the Council of State Governments reported on "Federal Grant-in-Aid Requirements Impeding State Administration." [9] A few selections will be instructive:

Florida. A public health nurse, financed from the special heart fund, is not supposed to render aid to cancer and tuberculosis patients even when they are in a household she is visiting.

Wisconsin. The Children's Bureau requires there be no more than 60 cases per child welfare caseworker. The state agency previously adopted a more sophisticated measurement of work which was not based on head counts. The state's standard is as high or higher than the federal, yet must be translated into federal terms. The five-to-one ratio of workers to supervisors does not take into account the fact that a BA social worker with no experience requires much more supervision than an MSW worker with five years' experience. The Bureau also requires that the person in charge of staff development have a master's degree in social work, although the state agency has determined that an educational degree would qualify a person just as well.

Pennsylvania. Each of the various grant programs for construction, such as Appalachia, Hill-Burton, mental retardation, and community mental health centers, has its own restrictions which often make it impossible to locate in the same facilities various services which should be together for most effective and efficient operation.

Georgia. State law allows travelers reimbursement for meals if travel away from the official station is in excess of three hours. The federal government, however, will not reimburse Civil Defense travel unless in excess of ten hours.

Vermont. The population criteria for community mental-health centers effectively prevent a rural population over a widely scattered area from receiving greatly needed mental-health facilities.

Washington. Handbook Transmittal No. 76 from the Bureau of Family Services, HEW, requires that by July 1, 1966, state plans under Titles I, IV, X, and XIV must provide for a simplified or a single standard for computing assistance grants. The federal requirements would operate to the detriment of many public assistance recipients, reducing the number of items now utilized in computing the grants. To simplify, the state must either use the highest standard, which it cannot afford, or use an average, which would result in cutting grants for some recipients and increasing grants for others. In addition, simplification would inequitably give a family with four teenage children the same money for food and clothing as a family with four small children. Simplification is presumed to reduce the high percentage of erroneous determinations of grants. This does not take into account the use in some states of data-processing equipment.

Kentucky. State agencies are having problems providing technical people to fill positions in the fast-moving, fast-changing federally-sponsored health programs. Present federal merit-system regulations concerning state merit systems are far too antiquated and cumbersome in methods of examination, certification, and appointment to supply qualified people in these programs.

Michigan. During the recent constitutionally mandated reorganization of the executive branch of state government, the governor urged maximum use of unclassified positions at policy levels. This was done quite uniformly throughout the nineteen new principal departments which were established. However, federal officials declined authority requested to establish two unclassified deputy directors in the Department of Social Service. There is a question whether such positions can be established even if paid entirely from state funds.

New York. Under the Vocational Education Act of 1963, funds are appropriated for six major purposes—secondary education, presecondary, adult, education of the handicapped, construction of facilities, and ancillary services. Federal reports, however, require annual reports of expenditures, not only according to these categories but also by subprogram areas, agriculture, distributive education, fishery, home economics, health, office technology, and trades and industry, within each of the six major purposes. Thus, fifty-four individual fiscal reports must be prepared and filed regarding expenditure of funds under the Vocational Education Act at both state and local levels. This takes weeks of staff time, both professional and nonprofessional.

New Mexico. The Public School Finance Division of the Department of Finance and Administration has over-all budgetary and accounting authority in the public-school area. This agency is best organized to administer federal funds for public-school purposes, but cannot do so under the single-agency requirement. Thus, New Mexico public schools must keep two sets of books in order to report separately to the Department of Education on use of federal funds and to report on all funds to the Public School Finance Division.

A Midwestern state department of education official, explaining his point of view, summed up all such impediments picturesquely. "We spend 60 per cent of our time educating the children of the state," he said, "and the other 40 per cent trying to educate the U.S. Office of Education to the special problems of our state. We don't begrudge the time it takes, not really. What gets us down is that the Office of Education has so many slow learners that it truly taxes our teaching skills."

A Western state welfare director thinks a review of "state plans and proposals by federal program and budget technicians with absolutely no knowledge of local problems leads to totally unrealistic appraisals in Washington. The legal staff reviews the welfare programs again and they have a veto on legal grounds. They don't, though, suggest legal alternatives to achieve the goals."

The defects cited in the complaints are not just a matter of irritation. They defeat the purpose and intent of Congress. They reduce the chance of success. They destroy initiative. They make the problem solving, already difficult enough, incalculably more difficult. And sometimes they make grant-in-aid projects look like foolish waste.

The town of Truro on Cape Cod, Massachusetts, was the site of a project under the Highway Beautification Act of 1965. A stretch of highway overlooking marsh, heather, dune, and ocean has been "beautified" by the planting of various non-indigenous trees and shrubs such as purple-flowering crabs, Australian pine, Japanese black pine, and forsythia, with an expanse of wood chips to cover the sand underneath. A local paper called it a "federal campaign to save Truro from looking like Truro" and says the project is "something like starting an anti-poverty program in Grosse Point, Michigan." [10]

Attempts to find out why a site with such native beauty was chosen elicited a general response that the money under the federal program had to be allocated by a certain date or it would revert to the federal treasury, and since work was already under way for erosion control there—why not beautify it also? "Which, of course, is a helluva way to run a program," said the newspaper. There should have been some way to use these funds to meet a useful highway need, without being tempted into such unplanned projects. Maybe the money could have been used in conjunction with the National Park Service, which is spending other sums to return much of the Truro area to its natural growth and terrain. Certainly such piecemeal granting of funds is a poor way to determine the priorities for spending public money. One great fault with the grand-in-aid approach is that priorities are reordered to suit the money available, forcing states to meet grants instead of meeting problems.

Another cause for concern is the lack of coordination between the federal agency and state government which trickles down to pollute the local efforts. Governor Daniel J. Evans of Washington told us this story:

Recently the Economic Development Administration funded a small sewage disposal plant near Seattle, rather than working with us and the Seattle Metropolitan area to require the community to join the area-wide sewerage system. This reinforced the fractionated local government system while at the same time other federal programs were trying to get local communities to consolidate efforts.

In spite of all the legislation passed in the last four years involving the national government in sweeping new interests and extending and deepening the old interests, there remains, to use a popular word, a gap. This is the gap between the view Congress has of the need to be met, and molding and administering a program which gets to the source of that need. Congress authorizes a program; the department or agency charged with the responsibility then draws up guidelines for it, usually, but not always, in harmony with congressional intent. But after that, in actual operation the program can be almost wholly removed from legislative intent by the individual interpretation of the guidelines by a fifth-echelon review which can effectively stall a project for many months.

It is not simply that the states should not be unduly burdened in receiving assistance. The objectives of Congress cannot be attained unless state government is allowed the freedom to add a creative part. Nor is a state helped, as Congress intends, if it must abandon needs in order to match funds for objectives less needed. The restructuring of our federal-state-local relationship is a profound need. And it can be done. It is not that the states, in drawing attention to the awkwardness and confusion, are looking the gift horse in the mouth. Rather it is that the objectives of the federal grant program will not be attained if the states are reduced to mere administrative arms of national programs.

1. *Cimarron,* Radio-Keith-Orpheum, January, 1931, starring Richard Dix, Irene Dunne, Edna Mae Oliver, Estelle Taylor.
2. Address by William G. Colman, "Creative Federalism—The Facts of Life," to the Conference on Public Administration, University of Oregon, Eugene, Oregon, September 7, 1966.
3. Howard Pyle, "Highway Safety," *The Book of the States, 1966–1967,* Vol. XVI, (Chicago: The Council of State Governments, 1966), p. 322. These rates are per 100 million miles of travel.
4. Eric Berne, *Games People Play, The Psychology of Human Relationships,* (New York: Grove Press, Inc., 1964), pp. 50–58, 104–105.
5. Morton Grodzins, "The Federal System," in *Goals for Americans,* Report of the President's Commission on National Goals, (Englewood Cliffs, New Jersey: Prentice-Hall, Inc., 1960), p. 265.
6. U.S., Congress, Senate, Subcommittee on Intergovernmental Relations of The Committee on Government Operations, *Catalog of Federal Aids to State and Local Governments,* 88th Cong., 2d. Sess., 1964; *Supplement January 4, 1965,* 89th Cong., 1st Sess., 1965; and *Second Supplement, January 10, 1966,* 89th Cong., 2d Sess., 1966, as reported in Norman Beckman, "For a New Perspective in Federal-State Relations," *State Government,* Vol. XXXIX, (Autumn, 1966), p. 262.
7. Letter from Lloyd Omdahl, Commissioner, North Dakota Tax Department, March 28, 1966.
8. Daniel J. Elazar, "The States and the Nation," in Herbert Jacob and Kenneth N. Vines, (eds.), *Politics in the American States,* (Boston: Little, Brown & Co., 1965), p. 468.
9. The Council of State Governments, *Federal Grant-in-Aid Requirements Impeding State Administration,* (Chicago: The Council of State Governments, 1966), pp. 7–12, 14, 17–18.
10. *The Cape Codder,* (Orleans, Massachusetts), August 25, 1966, p. 20.

CHAPTER X

States Need the Federal Power

The national government cannot effectively reach its goals without the power of the states.

The states cannot serve all their people without the power of the national government.

The city cannot overcome its problems without the power of the national government plus the power of the state.

The national and state governments cannot do their duty by the city residents without the power of the city government.

If all these propositions are true, and it seems to me they are beyond reasonable dispute, then some of the time-honored myths about American federalism are out of date. The governments are all in the same boat, tossed by the same waves and dependent on each others' paddles. When any one fails to row, they all move more slowly, and the waves become more dangerous for all.

Government is no longer merely to be tolerated as a necessary evil, but is regarded as both a protector and benefactor of the citizen who daily depends upon it for ever more and more costly services. He expects, and properly so, that these services will be efficiently administered. No one level or unit of government, acting alone, is capable of supplying all of his wants and needs . . . this means that, for virtually every important governmental function, there is a shared responsibility in our federal system." [1]

The adequacy of the states raises questions about the entire federal system and its total ability to handle the problems of our society and environment. The national government needs the power of the states. It cannot afford to see them scuttled. Neither can the states go it alone. They need the power of the national government.

The word *power*, as we discuss the capacity of governments, is not an apt word. It connotes coercive force. Government by force is obviously not the conscious goal of Americans. Capacity to act, or strength to accomplish the democratic purposes of its citizens, is the kind of power we need to build. The capacity of the states, of local governments, of the national government, is a proper subject of debate. It is necessary to banish the illusion that there is only a limited capacity available. Federalism is not premised on a single pot of power, to be ladled out so much to each bowl —local, state, federal—according to some preconceived plan. Max Ways stated it well:

In the long American dialogue over states' rights, it has been tacitly assumed that the total amount of power was constant and, therefore, any increase in federal power diminished the power of the states and/or the people. Creative federalism starts from the contrary belief that total power—private and public, individual and organizational—is expanding very rapidly. As the range of conscious choice widens, it is possible to think of vast increases of federal government power that do not encroach upon or diminish any other power. Simultaneously, the power of states and local governments will increase; the power of private organizations, including businesses, will increase; and the power of individuals will increase.[2]

In the last thirty-five years a general expansion of governmental activities has increased the power or, better, the capacity to provide a higher standard of life. The citizens, in vote after vote, have called for a broader, more activist role for government—at all levels and in all branches. They have moved from the days of looking at separate governments with distinctly separate duties and functions. They are not surprised to find all governments working on the same project. They seem to expect their governments to share responsibility.

When we are tempted to find fault with grants-in-aid and with sharing of responsibilities which belong essentially to the states, we should remember that the people have confirmed and supported a system of mixed government. But it is also important to remember that attitudes of the people who insist on the programs do not, at the same time, condone the inefficiency of administration. The complaints about over-standardization, unbending guidelines, the narrow scope of some grants, the inconsistent planning and reporting requirements are mostly justified. But complaints about excesses and bureaucratic fiddle-faddle do not argue persuasively against all standards and reasonable uniformity. So, to tote fair, both sides of the argument have validity. The evidence is not all one way. There is a good case to be made that the various grant programs, even with the strings, have been the mainstay of a highly effective system of federal government. It has been a system ever responsive to the needs of the people, constantly increasing the quality of the services, and testing the approaches from different angles and with diverse probes.

That we have overused the concept, with too many programs in confused arrangement, cannot be denied. But, on balance, there have been many benefits.

Citizens who move from state to state, as required by our economy and industrial complex, expect to find at least substantially the same type and degree of services—schools, hospitals, roads, and libraries, to name a few. When the national

grants were provided for particular needs, one purpose was
to achieve reasonable levels of service in all parts of the
country. Inevitably standards, as one of the strings to a grant,
have been superfluous in some states, requiring a lower quality of service than that already performed. In others, the
grants have indeed jacked up the minimum level of service,
a plus factor and one of the reasons the state took the grant
in the first place.

These standards have benefited not only those who moved,
but those who stayed put. Primarily because of the national
grants, there has been a change in velocity in these programs,
and a substantial improvement in quality. While I do not
agree with him in detail, it is worth passing on what a New
Jersey newsman told us: "The best-run programs are those
in which the federal government rules dominate."

The grant programs have also had some effect in making
possible services in parts of the country where the tax base
is small. To many, this has seemed merely robbing the pros-
perous states and individuals and turning over the receipts
to the poor states and the weak. To the cynical observer it
may even appear that a new Robin Hood has appeared. But
in fact, the wealth of our country and the resources that are
used to create the wealth are so intertwined that basic questions can be raised over just which government deserves to
receive and spend the tax receipts. As people and industry
cluster along our coasts, these states benefit from new revenue resources. The movement is out of the agricultural
areas, leaving those states with fewer resources. Yet we must
not forget that it is the great productive agricultural heart-
land of our nation, even with its declining population and
taxable resources, which makes it possible for so much of our
economy to be diverted to nonagricultural effort. The equal-
izing effect of federal grants does, therefore, support the
basic strength of our country rather than undermine it. In

fact, future needs will undoubtedly call for more equalization rather than less.

One recurring argument is that inflexible standards and procedures of grant programs reduce the flexibility of state government. The states are many times unduly restricted in the ways they might best develop particular programs. I am not at all certain, however, that their flexibility, or options for action, has not been promoted in a broader sense. For money, even with strings, breeds flexibility. More choices are available in the supermarket than in a country store. In this larger sense, the grant programs obviously increase the options of state government in meeting the demands upon it. At the same time, supplemental federal monies often multiply the flexibility of previously established state programs.

A large and growing number of national grant programs have as their objective innovations in public services or facilities . . . [especially the] multiplication of small grant sums authorized as "seedmonies" to focus attention on a needed public service through a demonstration of new techniques. . . . New ideas, new methods, and new arrangements are being encouraged. . . .[3]

Grant funds have enhanced state flexibility in yet another way. The availability of matching money has frequently enabled state legislatures to initiate programs they would otherwise have found impossible. It is tough to sell a legislature on using money to try out a new idea. There are so many demands for available funds to expand old programs or catch up old shortcomings. Available federal money has given legislators the urge to act. It has also given them the excuse to act, a way to explain their vote—"Here were funds we couldn't afford to lose." And many beneficial starts have been made on this excuse. The programs have also given the governor and the executive branch some of the same kind of flexibility.

Flexibility in options has led to the program for aid to the migrants, developed under the Economic Opportunity Program in California; has given support to the startling display of creativeness in urban renovation and renewal in New Haven, Connecticut; has allowed states such as Vermont to develop a new, regional definition of local government under a grant for state planning; has enabled school boards throughout the country to experiment with new methods of reaching children under the Elementary and Secondary Education Act of 1965; has allowed states and localities to try new and exciting ways to bring a newly retrained man and an available job together under the manpower and economic-opportunity programs; is stimulating the states to take a part in their own cultural and artistic resources under the National Endowment for the Arts and Humanities program; and so on down a long-continuing list. It is still the local and state leaders who must pick up the ball and run with it—and the evidence is that they have done so. But it is fair to remember that much of the flexibility was stimulated by national funds.

As a people we are faced with conditions generated by our rapid urban and suburban growth which require our immediate attention before they are totally out of hand. Decayed and decaying city centers, congested traffic, open areas, smoke, recreation, rapid transit, and housing are words that bring a cold sweat to officials and administrators with any responsibility for cities. The problems they suggest challenge the resources of every level of government, and every level must participate if our cities are to be livable. The states must play a drastically increased role. Most of them will. But there is not a state with a sizable city that believes the job can be done without an increase in national grants and funds.

The inevitability of national aid in no way diminishes the inevitability of continuing state action. While the states cannot perform many of their duties without the assistance of the national government, neither can the national government do what it must without the assistance of the state governments. Cooperation is basic in a federal system. It is necessary in our tremendous and diverse country. That is why we are struggling to increase it.

One example of the necessity for this interdependence lies in the present racial unrest and the surge for equal rights and opportunities. Recent civil-rights legislation has broken down many of the legal barriers. The continuing advance must now be found in state and community action, not so much legal as general. With time, we can begin to erase the legacy of the Southern cotton field and the Northern ghetto. Federal legislation and court decisions can topple the legal barriers, and national grants can help in supporting community action, but only state and local concern and action can help bring about the full human understanding essential to the health of our society.

There can be some consolation for those who urge an increase in the vitality of state governments. The partnership is mutual. For, as William Anderson says, "Political power, like electricity, does not run all in one direction." [4] The states still influence their own changing destiny. Anderson clarifies the point:

Does not the federal-aid system, by giving state agencies the power to administer functions in which there is a national interest, actually give the states considerable control over national policy and effectiveness in the area, control which they otherwise would not have, in addition to giving the states the extra funds? . . . In short, as administrators of federal programs under grant-in-aid the state governments have acquired something in the nature of an added check upon the national administration.[5]

In the wide view of history, the states have brought focus

to the federal system. The natoinal government is positioned to look at problems and programs in broad, general, aggregate terms of national policy and purpose. Local communities see the world in narrow, particular, individual terms, and should. This is their beauty. The states, as regions—territorial entities—are the means by which these two points of view can be brought together in the service of the citizens.

1. W. Brooke Graves, "Creative Federalism's Challenge to the States," unpublished paper prepared for The Committee on Economic Development, July 5, 1966, p. 66.
2. Max Ways, "Creative Federalism and the Great Society," *Fortune* (January, 1966), p. 122.
3. Selma Mushkin and Robert F. Adams, "Emerging Patterns of Federalism," *National Tax Journal,* Vol. XIX, (September, 1966), p. 235.
4. William Anderson, *The Nation and the States, Rivals or Partners?,* (Minneapolis: University of Minnesota Press, 1955), pp. 203-204.
5. *Ibid.*

CHAPTER XI

Competition Keeps Us Free

Lewis Mumford recently observed that the New York sky-scrapers are "just glass-and-metal filing cabinets," and the high-rise apartments, filled with "filing-card people, . . . are dehumanized forms as dwellings. They reduce human beings to ciphers; they create feelings of impotence and unimportance. They make living just another aspect of the regimentation of business life." [1] There is danger that ours may become an age of depersonalized men, where the citizen is identified by a string of numbers, programmed daily by computers, and occasionally bent or spindled by a careless programmer or a faulty transistor in a basement somewhere in Washington.

Many forces have shaped this generation, and some of the symptoms can be traced to changing patterns of government. When the depression of the 1930s plunged the nation into deep economic crisis, action was needed. Our people turned to Washington, and Washington responded magnificently. Our national government sought the most practical way to help a people suddenly helpless when banks failed, factories closed, and millions lost their jobs. The situation demanded action in bold and innovative programs, with quick results. To meet this demand the New Deal broke old patterns of aloof permissiveness and set up new patterns of control over the activities of banks, brokers, businesses, and individuals. It nationalized government as never before.

And so began a romance. Washington had the solution to all our biting social problems. As the action progressed, the romance of the New Deal brought further disenchantment with the apparently feeble states. Many were convinced that state interference in national programs would cheat individuals of their rightful benefits or deny them their civil liberties. State participation in federal programs would mar the uniformity of these programs, make their administration cumbersome, and consequently reduce their effectiveness. The pragmatic approach of the old liberals who had always believed in individual rights gradually became an ideology of centralism. For some, it was an ex post facto justification, but for others it became the new faith.

Now there are nagging doubts. Predictions of the withering or death of state government seem somehow at odds with old Jeffersonian principles and the basic new-world concern for the individual and individualism. Many thoughtful people have begun to have ambivalent feelings about the impersonal nature of highly centralized government and its effect on the character of our society.

For whatever else our age may be known, it will be remembered for increased organization that tends to make the individual something like a cog in a machine. For the individual, this means peril to his liberties. The national government surely has no such intentions, but it is moving toward ever-greater centralization and mechanization. In a system of centralized bureaus endowed with the authority to interpret the intentions of Congress and thus make many final decisions that affect the individual, the individual and his personal liberty seem simply a hindrance to efficiency. With the carrot of grants-in-aid and the stick of deprival of funds, bureaus can lead us almost unawares into a coercive society. In a recent speech, Richard Goodwin, former aide to Presidents Kennedy and Johnson, discussed the coercive society into which we seem to be moving:

We will have to reshape the historic relationships of our Federal structure so as not to be completely dependent on Washington for comfort, help, and skill. . . . The problems are far too huge and varied to be solved from the top.

Moreover, to attempt it is to strip people in communities and states of the chance to share in the solution of the great problems of society. It is essential to our spiritual health to develop structures which give people a chance to share in the American enterprise.

We, who have often looked to Washington for protection of human rights, must increase our guard against the coercive society. It is the nature of power to resent opposition to its exercise. That resentment is multiplied as power grows. When those who have such power are also convinced of the wisdom and beneficence of their views, then freedom is in danger. . . . Already wiretapping, bugging, and manifold invasions of privacy are growing, I believe, far beyond the present knowledge of any of us. . . .[2]

Recently the U.S. Budget Bureau made a proposal for a national data center, suggesting a plan whereby twenty federal agencies and departments that now guard their own data would feed a centralized computer. According to Cornelius F. Gallagher, chairman of the House Subcommittee on the Invasion of Privacy, the pooled information could include a man's schooling, grades, military service, personality traits, credit rating, income, employment, and "practically any other aspect of his life." [3]

Vance Packard, author of *The Naked Society* and other books, testified at a hearing on the proposed computer bank: "My own hunch is that Big Brother, if he ever comes to these United States, may turn out not to be a greedy power seeker, but rather a relentless bureaucrat obsessed with efficiency." [4]

Computers are not bad. They are neutral. Like the surgeon's knife that can be used either to cut out a cancer or slit a throat, computers can be used to add either to freedom or to restriction. They offer vast new powers to government in dealing with the complex and difficult problems of analysis, record keeping, and projection of future needs.

Computers form only one battalion in the technological

army jeopardizing self-reliance and individualism. We are going to need to be watchful for ways to establish proper restraints and defenses to protect against abusive application of the technology which can so easily be used for coercion or invasion of privacy.

Overorganization and centralization are threats. But they can be combated with a theory familiar in American life, competition. Governmental competition may come into its own in the age of technology. Political scientists call it the concept of countervailing governments: you match a bear with strong jaws against a wolf with sharp claws.

From America's earliest days her people have been aware of the dangers of arbitrary power, whether in government, institutions, or big business. Our favorite device for thwarting arbitrary power has been competition under law.

We must have competition among governmental levels for many reasons. Stimulation for creative improvement is one. But the urgent reason is to defend ourselves against the possible abuses of centralized power. Abuses will not come because of technology. They will come from the human use of machines, and the human mind itself, especially as the American tax patterns shift more and more money, talent, and raw power to Washington.

Our forebears built our system of government on the theory that we must have checks and balances at the seat of power. Many of them had fled the persecution of central governments in other countries. Traditionally most Americans have felt that a single center of power is potentially dangerous. They have always asked who will hear the individual's complaints. Where will the political muscle come from to support the private citizen and groups of citizens who may have valid objections to the actions of government, as well as those with grievances that might not seem valid to the majority?

Where will the countervailing force come from? By what other means can the citizens stand up against a central government vastly stronger than any other? What other political power can be called upon if individual liberties are ignored in the name of over-all efficiency? If the national government forgets, who can call it to task?

Contrary to the arguments of those who insist that the states are finished, there is only one answer to these questions. The states must develop the capacity through renewed and potent state government.

Why select the states for this role?

Constitutionally they form the backbone of our federal system, the only other governments with a basis in the United States Constitution. The states are not creatures of the Congress, and are not administrative subdivisions, but exist by the fundamental authority of the land. They cannot be shunted around, or have their structure altered, or be summarily dismissed, as can units of government created by legislative or executive acts of the national government. In a word, they are the only governments as constitutionally secure as the national government.

In addition, the political role of the states places them in the warp and woof of our national political fabric. There is no other power able to withstand the ultimate political strength of the national government in its slide toward domineering all government activities. Unless the states develop their own force, we may ultimately have only one seat of political power. There is little in history to make that a comforting thought.

American federalism has been consistent with the values that gave life and vitality to our Revolution. As one author has put it in describing *The Federalist Papers:*

The doctrine of *The Federalist* is that popular government, with its essential accompaniments of freedom of opinion and the right to disagree, depends upon no single agency or protection. Rather it rests upon multiple protections, plural safeguards, or, as Madison puts it, "auxiliary precautions." [5]

As the states provide the auxiliary precaution against the abuse of power by the national government, so the national government stands as the auxiliary precaution against abuse by the states. As the states must safeguard the individual from coercion and invasion of privacy by the national government, the national government must assure the individual of the rights guaranteed him by the United States Constitution and protect him against transitory passions that run counter to American liberty and deny our belief that justice resides in the human heart.

To abandon the states, to seek answers to social questions without them, is to misunderstand our system and undermine it. To build them up, to involve them to their utmost capacity, is to strengthen our system in all its endeavors and protections. This may keep the fires of tension burning between the nation and the states—but it is this very fire which has propelled our system from the birth of the nation.

Thomas Jefferson wrote that the only way the states can avoid the abuse of national power is "to strengthen the State governments, and as this cannot be done by any change in the federal constitution . . . it must be done by the States themselves. . . ." [6]

---

1. *The New York Times*, March 22, 1967, pp. 49, 95.
2. Speech by Richard Goodwin, to the National Board Meeting of Americans for Democratic Action, Washington, D.C., September 17, 1966.
3. *The New York Times*, July 27, 1966.
4. *Ibid.*
5. Benjamin Fletcher Wright (ed.), *The Federalist* by Alexander Hamilton, James Madison and John Jay, (Cambridge: Harvard University Press, 1961), p. 84.
6. Letter from Thomas Jefferson, Monticello, Virginia, to Samuel Kercheval, July 12, 1816, in Edward Dunbauld, (ed.), *The Political Writings of Thomas Jefferson*, (Indianapolis: Bobbs-Merrill Company, Inc., 1955), p. 113.

CHAPTER XII

States Working Together

A noted newspaper columnist asked me several months ago why it would not be possible for all of the New England states to merge into one. "It won't work for a lot of reasons," I said, "but the simplest is that they are not going to give up ten of their twelve U.S. senators."

"Well, why wouldn't it be worked so the new state of New England could have twelve senators?"

"Because," I told him, "California wouldn't go along with that." Neither would New Hampshire, Maine, or Vermont, where there still exists a fierce sense of state pride. Listen to these words of Ethan Allen inscribed on the walls of the capitol of Vermont: "I am as determined to preserve the Independence of Vermont as Congress is that of the Union and rather than fail I will retire with my hardy green mountain boys into the caverns of the mountains and make war on all mankind."

Merger is a moot question, although some functions of state government cannot be performed adequately by one state moving alone. These relate to problems that are not necessarily national problems even though they cross state borders. The practical answer, rather than merger of states or federal action, is that where joint efforts are needed, states can develop cooperative answers, often through the use of interstate compacts.

The interstate compact is a legislative contract between two or more states providing "a new dimension for state power. It permits the states to take continuing cooperative action in fields where they cannot act effectively or do not wish to act alone, fields which might fall by default to the federal power if not occupied through the initiative of the states." [1] The United States Supreme Court has interpreted the powers of these compact agencies broadly, so they "may operate as arms of state governments under a collective delegation of legislative power from each state involved." [2]

The leaders of the New England states have already recognized that their region can best handle many of its problems in a coordinated, multi-state effort. The New England Governors' Conference meets in several one-day meetings during the year for discussion and action on a variety of common problems. This regional approach spans a number of activities, as Governor John H. Chafee of Rhode Island has pointed out: "We have some twenty-eight regional governmental groups, among which are the State Police Administration, Water Pollution Control Commission, and Motor Vehicles officials." [3] In the summer of 1966 the New England states adhered to forty-three compacts, ten of which had to do with boundaries. In one of their most successful ventures, these states coordinated their work in higher education under the New England Board of Higher Education, a compact agency established in 1955. "Specialized programs at one state's university are open to students from other states at no extra cost. Over 400 students a year are interchanged by the board, whose activities have been quite successful, although it has not reached its full potential." [4] The smallest of the compacts is the New Hampshire–Vermont School District Compact, which authorizes the children of Norwich, Vermont, to go to school across the river in Hanover, New Hampshire, and sets the formula for joint support.[5]

Other regions have taken a similar tack. In 1949 the Southern governors established the Southern Regional Education Board. This compact, which was the prototype for the other regional education compacts, provides the structure for a regional system of professional and graduate education for fifteen Southern states. This cooperative effort arranges education for about 1,100 students each year in some thirty graduate and professional fields, and involves some twenty-five universities. Under this system the Alabama student in library science attends the University of North Carolina, and the North Carolina veterinary student attends the University of Georgia. It represents the annual expenditure of about $1,700,000 in state funds, plus grants from private foundations and federal agencies.[6] A more important result may be that money is not spent for competing faculty, duplicate facilities are not built in neighboring states, and therefore funds go further in upgrading higher education all over the South. Most important, the board has furnished impetus and leadership for constant improvement. A similar compact agency joins thirteen Western states under the Western Interstate Commission for Higher Education.

Interstate compacts can serve a variety of purposes. The state of Maryland operates the Port of Baltimore, but imagine the confusion if New York ran one side and New Jersey the other side of the Port of New York. By interstate compact in 1922, the two states created the Port of New York Authority, one of the country's most successful compact agencies. The authority, as an instrument of both states, and on behalf of each state, operates bridges, airports, tunnels, piers, heliports, and bus terminals, while directing the harbor activities and promoting the development of the Port of New York, including at present the building of a $500-million world trade center.

Because river basins know not the lines of states, compacts for the control and use of rivers are numerous. There are compacts for the control and preservation of the Delaware River (four states and the U.S. government), the Potomac River (four states, the District of Columbia, and the United States government), the Colorado River (four states), the New England rivers (seven states), and the Ohio River (eight states). The Ohio River Valley Water Sanitation Commission was organized in 1948 to control future pollution and to abate existing pollution of the waters of the Ohio River Valley from the headwaters in New York and Virginia to Illinois and Kentucky where it flows into the Mississippi River. While the commission reported in March, 1967, that it had by no means satisfied the ultimate aim to restore the wholesomeness of the waters, the pollution-control program "is well along to completion" and "at all major and most minor sources of sewage discharge communities have shouldered the complex task of acquiring treatment-plant locations, installing the interceptor sewers and pumping equipment to bring all waste waters to these sites, and constructing treatment works and sludge disposal facilities."[7]

The states have long exchanged information and ideas through a number of organizations. The most significant association of states and state officials is the Council of State Governments. With financial support from the states, it conducts valuable research, and serves as the authoritative clearinghouse for state governments. Since the 1920s it has kept track of what each of the states is doing. It serves as the secretariat of ten organizations of state officials including the National Governors' Conference and the National Legislative Conference as well as the Conferences of Chief Justices, Attorneys General, and Lieutenant Governors. Under the early guidance of Henry Toll and Frank Bane, and with the continued leadership of its executive director, Brevard Crihfield, the Council is a valuable source for information, for recommended statutes and activities, and for technical advice on specialized problems. The states have adopted uniform laws relating to certain subjects, in order to keep pace with the mobility of America. This cooperation is not achieved by compact, but simply by individual enactment in the states that desire to cooperate. The National Conference of Commissioners on Uniform State Laws has promoted successful adoption by most states of a uniform commercial code, the

Uniform Negotiable Instruments Law, the Uniform Ware-house Receipts Act, and the Uniform Narcotics Drug Act, and many states have enacted nearly a hundred other uniform acts.[8] These acts generally involve transactions between citizens of different states, business activities running across state lines, or law-enforcement procedures; and they make general national laws unnecessary, which in many cases could not be constitutionally enacted anyway.

One promising cooperative experiment today is the Appalachian program. It is an innovative approach to a common problem, the lack of economic development in mountain country. This is a diverse area, ranging from southern New York State to northern Alabama and Mississippi, which includes some pockets of prosperity. At the instigation of the governors of these states and by Congressional Act, the federal government and thirteen states have entered into a joint venture "to assist the region in meeting its special problems, to promote its economic development and to establish a framework for joint federal and state efforts toward providing the basic facilities essential to its growth and attacking its common problems and meeting its common needs on a coordinated and concerted regional basis." [9] There are similar regional programs authorized by Congress in "Ozarkia" (Arkansas, Missouri, Oklahoma), "Four Corners" (Arizona, Colorado, New Mexico, Utah), the Upper Great Lakes (the northernmost portions of Michigan, Minnesota, and Wisconsin), the Coastal plains (Georgia, North Carolina, South Carolina), and the New England states. These programs place the major burden on the states and the governors, in planning, in policy making, in decision making, and in administering the multi-state programs. Each state approaches the program differently and at different levels of sophistication—but this is a strength, not a weakness. It builds diversity where it is needed and modifies a monolithic approach to varied problems.

Governor Calvin L. Rampton of Utah reasoned:

If government must become involved in a problem, it should be at the level closest to the problem but on a geographic basis large enough to obtain a solution.

There is a gray area between what the federal government can handle and the state governments, and it seems to be regional. If the states do not enter this field, the federal government will flow in.

We want the cooperation of the federal government because of its greater resources; but we want the direction to come from here.[10]

A dramatic development in cooperative state action was the creation last year of the nationwide Compact for Education. The idea was first suggested by James B. Conant,[11] whose distinguished studies of American education have contributed many improvements and reforms. In seeking to determine how educational policy was shaped in America he concluded that it wasn't being done at all except in a totally unorganized way. Dr. Conant felt that education was too important to be left to the haphazard chance of unconnected local and state efforts and too complex to be left to a single guiding national hand. He concluded that if at least fifteen states, representative of all parts of the nation, were to join together by compact for this purpose, they could provide the authentic and legally based organization for looking to the states' future in educational policy.

The Study of American States undertook the task of mobilizing the officials of the states and leaders in education. In May, 1965, we convened the first meeting in Washington, inviting representatives of every conceivable organization whose purpose was related to education, plus legislators and governors. Out of this meeting came a drafting committee, made up of representatives of the associations with legal duties in education, such as the Association of Chief State School Officers. With Mitchell Wendell, of the Council of State Governments, as our authoritative specialist and draftsman, we worked all summer on the documents and legal requirements. By late summer the specific proposals had been presented to numerous interested organizations, including the National Governors' Conference, which voted unanimous approval.

In September, at Kansas City, a conference was held for further discussion and adoption, amendment or rejection of the proposals. Each governor had been invited to send the delegates authorized by the proposed compact, comprising the governor, legislators, and lay and professional educational leaders, public and private. Surprisingly every state was represented, as were Puerto Rico and the territories, and nineteen governors were there in person. The group debated, improved, and adopted the compact, bylaws, and plan of organization, and elected an interim steering committee with Governor Chafee of Rhode Island as first chairman.[12] By June, 1966, when the first full and formal meeting was held, thirty-seven states had become members of the compact. The organization, called the Education Commission of the States, has a home in Denver, Colorado, where its second full meeting was held in May, 1967, after a year of gearing up and starting studies. There is a full-time staff and initial support funds have been provided by Carnegie Corporation and Danforth Foundation. Beginning January 1, 1968, the member states will pay the ongoing expenses on a formula basis. I have gone into some detail because it seems to me that this is a remarkable example of the readiness of state government and its leaders to take up their responsibilities. No other compact covers such a broad slice of state responsibilities, and none was ever embraced so quickly and warmly.

The compact gives the states an office for developing alternatives for policy decisions, which ultimately, and in any event, are to be made by local and state policy-making bodies. It furnishes the states with the best available information. It is a clearinghouse for ideas, and a forum for sharing experiences, improving performance, and debating goals.

The compact makes it possible for success to feed upon success, as ideas are more easily transmitted across state and regional lines.

Its unique feature is that it joins the political and professional forces in education across the nation to discuss what they can do in partnership for the advancement of education. Its purpose is to assure a constant confrontation between the political forces which must support education and the educators who must transform new funds into real achievements. For many educators, the meetings of the commission represented the first time they had talked to legislators without a hearing table in front of them; for governors and legislators, it was an opportunity to learn about educational advances all across the country and to measure their own state's performance against the accomplishments of others.

This compact arrangement does not delegate authority to act, as does, for example, the Port of New York compact. Dr. Conant spelled out its general purpose:

This is not a new mechanism for action—it is a new mechanism which may stimulate action state by state . . . stimulating action by providing the necessary information which is now not available in regard to many important problems . . . an approach which places no restraint on the states, but provides what the states need to act wisely.[13]

The agenda of the commission is broad and varied. It ranges from the potential of preschool training to the problems of postgraduate education; from the questions of training, retraining, selection, and certification of teachers to the possibilities of new techniques and new curricula; from the challenges presented by the large urban high schools to the prospects for the rural high school; from the alternatives for financing and administering our public schools to the role of our private schools—these and the many more subjects that need intensive study and action.

Education is both the end product and best hope of any

state government. The Education Commission is enabling the states to unite in the resolve to meet their responsibility to the quickening interest of the American people in the pursuit of educational excellence. The Compact for Education places the states in the forefront of that pursuit.

The convincing enthusiasm of the states for the Compact for Education furnished ample evidence of the eagerness of the states to move forward. But the states, or so we concluded over the course of our study, needed another kind of institution. One major weakness of the states is that governors and legislators, with the best intentions of improving the effectiveness of state government, frequently have difficulty knowing where they should start improvement and how they should go about it. Too often they are flying blind, without the charts on which to plot the course.

I wanted to find a way the states could cooperatively encourage each other to excellence. We tried to construct an organization with the ability to combine knowledge and action to bring focus, periodically, to every field of state government. We called this concept the Institute of the States. The Institute will provide a means by which the states can create their own incentives for action and provide themselves with the best information and thinking in the various areas of state responsibility. In a sense, the states will have a joint action committee and a state-created source of advice and guidance to governors, legislators, and administrators who want to accept the charge of leadership.

The Institute of the States will be directed by a small but distinguished board and have a staff of only two or three. This parent organization will suggest, create, promote, and organize satellite institutes for specifically assigned missions. There can be several in progress at any one time. These satellites will use every method available to promote improvement and stimulate action in their particular field of state government responsibility, be it constitutional reform, mental health, transportation, state taxes, conservation and recreation, or any one of several dozen other state functions.

Each satellite institute will be located on a campus of one of our great universities and have a limited life of two years. It will have a small staff and will be directed by a former governor. In this way the states can take advantage of the vast stores of knowledge in the academic world and put to good use the ideas, experience, and political acumen of former state leaders. By being collapsed in two years, the satellite institutes would not be concerned with promoting their own permanent position, would operate with a sense of urgency, and would be free to contend for improvement. Satellite institutes, working closely with governors and with state legislative leadership, will be able to draw together ideas, experience, and successful activities from all the states. They will be free to do battle with inertia, to think boldly and creatively, to criticize state effort or lack of it, to push, to prod, and to stay close to where the action is. Their goal is a short and productive life, creating new interest and starting new action.

A trial run of the idea, the prototype, is the Institute on State Programming for the Seventies, established in the spring of 1967 at the University of North Carolina at Chapel Hill with a Carnegie Corporation grant. It is headed by Jack M. Campbell, former governor of New Mexico. To advise him, he will have a committee of faculty members, and another committee made up of governors, former governors, legislators, state officials, local officials, and other citizens. The purposes of the Institute on State Programming are to look carefully at all current state planning devices; to gather and develop new ideas and methods such as those used by aerospace industries and other private businesses for advanced programming; and to illustrate by an educational campaign the need and benefits of long-range planning as an effective tool for governors, legislators, and administrators. Its hope is that the individual states will start the significant upgrading of the art of long-range planning, thereby developing a "guidance" system for the states. From time to time other institutes, on other campuses, with other governors, concerned with other subjects, can be started.

The Institute of the States will provide the states with a cooperative, built-in stimulus for action and a constant fount of refreshed ideas and approaches as they seek the initiative in expanding the effectiveness of state government.

Compacts and other cooperative arrangements, successful in so many cases, provide an alternative to national action on multi-state but non-national issues. It is not necessary to call on the federal government unless the people are unwilling to call on their state governments to deal with these special problems that spill over state lines. This could apply to urban subjects, to manpower training, to air pollution, to mass transportation, and to almost any other topic, and for almost any number of states.

There is, however, a danger that these could become too specialized, like many special districts of the past that now add to the confusion of local government. On the other hand, so could a multiplication of categorical programs by the national government. Neither, however, needs be approached so narrowly.

Interstate cooperation, like so many other programs that involve groupings of governments or cooperative endeavors, has grown slowly because some states felt that each of these arrangements was somehow a surrender of state sovereignty. Yet the most attractive feature of the interstate device is that it maintains state individuality, while allowing a group of states to make a more direct attack on problems that may have sources in many states.

Governor John Love of Colorado sees that "the next step that must be taken is up to the citizens of the various states. They must be made to recognize the attributes of interstate cooperation, and they must direct their elected officials to take part in interstate cooperation to preserve the integrity of state government." [14]

To create or take part in these cooperative arrangements requires, in most cases, no more than the initiative of the governors of the states involved. It is often an attractive alternative for the people, if they choose to summon state governments to service.

1. Richard H. Leach and Redding S. Sugg, Jr., *The Administration of Interstate Compacts*, (Baton Rouge: Louisiana State University Press, 1959), p. 6.
2. *Ibid.*, p. 13.
3. Speech by John H. Chafee, Governor of Rhode Island and Providence Plantations, to the Boston College Seminar at the Prudential Center, February 21, 1967.
4. *Ibid.*
5. *Interstate Compacts 1783-1966, A Compilation*, (Chicago: The Council of State Governments, 1966), pp. 79-80.
6. Leach and Sugg, *op. cit.*, pp. 202-203, and *Southern Regional Education Board '66 '67* (Atlanta: Southern Regional Education Board, 1966).
7. The Ohio River Valley Water Sanitation Commission, *Eighteenth Yearbook 1966*, (Cincinnati, 1967), p. 2.
8. Walter D. Malcolm, "Uniform State Laws," *Book of the States 1966-1967*, Vol. XVI, (Chicago: The Council of State Governments, 1966), p. 89.
9. U.S. Public Law 89-4.
10. *The Christian Science Monitor*, (Boston), September 13, 1966.
11. James B. Conant, *Shaping Educational Policy*, (New York: McGraw-Hill Book Company, 1964). See especially Chapter 5, "Toward a Nationwide Educational Policy," pp. 109-134.
12. Governor Charles L. Terry, Jr., of Delaware was elected chairman in June, 1966, and Governor Calvin L. Rampton of Utah succeeded him in May, 1967.
13. Speech by James B. Conant, President Emeritus, Harvard University, to the Planning Conference for the proposed Compact for Education, Kansas City, Missouri, September 29, 1965.
14. Letter from John Love, Governor of Colorado, August 5, 1966.

CHAPTER XIII

States Must Work Where People Live

"I haven't got time to fool with the state," the mayor of one of our ten great cities told the reporters at the airport as he was catching a plane to Washington.

The Mayor of Minneapolis said, "If you tried to identify the twenty-five spots of dynamic sparks, where cities are reaching out to meet the future, they would all be tied to federal programs."

The Mayor of Bremerton, Washington, "goes to Washington, D.C., a 2,400-mile safari, ten times for every single sixty-mile trip to Olympia," an observer notes.

The Mayor of Atlanta charged that the problems of metropolitan development are "totally foreign" to state government and the "major thrust of high idealism" to cope with these problems has come from the federal government.[1]

The constant indictment is that the states, or most of them, have not shown that they care enough about urban affairs, and are not attentive to the needs of the cities. The states, all of them, must find better ways of coming to the aid of their local governments if they expect to be working where the people are. I believe, though, that the picture of state neglect has been overdrawn by many analysts. The broadside criticism is unfair; the states have not been totally unconcerned. They have increased their intergovernmental grants and expenditures to local governments from $52 million in 1902 to $596 million in 1927, to $1.5 billion in 1938, to $3.3 billion in 1948, and to $14.2 billion in 1965. As a percentage of local general revenues, the rise has been from 6.1 per cent in 1902 to nearly 30 per cent in 1965.[2] As James A. Maxwell indicates, "state governments now provide a good slice of the finances of important functions of local government . . . and they give a good deal of direction as well. In some states centralization has gone further, with complete control of a function assumed by the state government."[3]

I do not insist that this increasing support has been sufficient, or that the states have provided all necessary assistance to the cities. What I do contend is that we have seen a crisis of responsibility at every level of government. Our people and our problems have been moving closer and closer together for many years, yet it is only recently that we have begun to recognize the consequences. As the crisis has risen, it is obvious that the states have not done enough, the cities have seemed paralyzed, and the national government has inaugurated as many wrong approaches as right solutions. The answers, however, will not be found by assessing blame, but by drawing together all our resources. Basically, we have not defined the crises correctly, and we have left to the cities problems they cannot solve.

It is no longer possible for the states to assert that all federal funds should be channeled through the states. The facts have long since disproved this argument. Federal assistance has been increasing for a generation. So many local functions are carried on in so many ways with money from the national tax sources that it is difficult, if not impossible, to catalogue everything being done, much less unwind and stop the process.

Paul N. Ylvisaker described in detail the national funds coming into Blue Earth County, Minnesota, twenty years ago. His conclusion was that "state and federal governments finance one-third of the cost of local government in Blue Earth County (1945), in addition to which they spend as much within the community as do all local units combined." The amount of federal funds involved was "clearly greater than that of the state." [4]

Some ten years later Morton Grodzins studied seven scattered small towns across the United States. He tells about the city manager of a Midwestern town who told an interviewer emphatically that he had nothing to do with federal programs and "never wanted to."

He was interrupted by a message from a radio receiver at his back; and in the next ten minutes he gave radio messages to a street maintenance crew, the chief of police, and a member of the fire department. He turned away from his business with the remark that he could never get his day's work done without the convenience of the short-wave two-way radio. The interviewer ventured the opinion that the system looked expensive as well as efficient. The manager said it was, but added with satisfaction: "Of course the Civil Defense Administration paid for most of it." The discovery of this Federal contact soon led to many others. [5]

Grodzins' study of government in Casa Grande, Arizona (situated between Phoenix and Tucson with a population in 1958 of about 9,000) found the hand of the national government, with checkbook, on every street corner. Some 3 per cent of the citizens were receiving welfare payments, administered by the county, but with mostly national and some state funds. A number received social security payments. A county public-health office used national funds for the treatment of tuberculosis, control of venereal diseases, nurses under the maternal and child-care program, polio vaccine, a contemplated study of mental health, and a county health center building, all "but samples of the national government's role in activities carried out in the city of Casa Grande by officers of Pinal County under the supervision of, and with funds partially supplied by, the state of Arizona."

The local office of the Arizona Employment Security Commission and the Casa Grande Community Hospital are two of numerous other connecting points with national funds. Federal contributions to the schools, considerable but not then substantial, included the free-lunch and milk program, special classes under the Smith–Hughes Act, some summer fellowships for teachers from the National Science Foundation, publications from the Department of Agriculture and the U.S. Office of Education, and reimbursement for teaching the Indian children attending high school, as well as a truck, radios, tools, stoves, dishwashers, and an outmoded Link Trainer from the distribution of federal surplus property.

A full quota of federally engineered local governments for agricultural purposes existed in Pinal County . . . the soil bank . . . guaranteed cotton prices . . . grants and loans for soil conservation. . . . The funds distributed through ASC programs represented the largest single expenditure by any government within the county, and of course had the most profound effect on the economy of the city.

Also reaching a substantial number of city residents were the Agriculture Extension Service programs in home economics through homemakers' clubs, the 4-H clubs, technical meetings, and home demonstrations. The inspections for industrial safety and the purity of food and drugs, examination to protect bank deposits, mail delivery, and drafting the young men are some of the other federal activities, in most of which the state participates to some degree. Almost everything mentioned essentially by-passes the regularly elected government of Casa Grande.

The main street is a "federally aided state highway." Some of the older WPA city streets are still in use. The chief of police has his autographed picture of J. Edgar Hoover and his diploma from the FBI National Police Academy, and the FBI laboratory is called on when needed. The jail was built with advice from the U.S. Bureau of Prisons, and federal prisoners were lodged there for short periods, for which compensation was paid to the city. "The first city planning in Casa Grande was made possible by Federal grants," obtained, incidentally, by the intervention of a private consulting firm. The town received from Washington a grant and a loan for the sewer system, a gift of the airport (surplus) and funds for its facilities, a transfer of a mountain park, twenty low-cost housing units, and the National Guard armory. These are only part of a long list.[6]

Casa Grande illustrates how intertwined with national programs is the trellis of local government. In the ensuing decade the intertwining has become even more complicated. By the end of 1966, the national government had more than fifty separate grant programs for local government, twelve of them passed by the Eighty-ninth Congress. To talk of the past success or failure of local government is to talk of the national government and its assistance for many years in almost every local function.

Over the past fifty years, the rapid growth of the cities has brought enormous demands for new and expanded services. Local governments, unable to answer these demands, began to look for help. The needs were so complex and so numerous that it was virtually impossible to convince a rural-oriented state legislature that it had a substantial urban duty. Then, too, the cities seemed to be governed during most of this century by political organizations which cared about the votes in the neighborhood but didn't see themselves as innovators of new programs. The office of the mayor, with some exceptions, was defensive in character, and the mayor's survival rested on his ability to hold coalitions together. The new suburbanite seldom saw the problems of the center city as his own; he only worked there. The Negroes and poor whites who were left had little consciousness of their power and little preparation for filling the vacated role of civic leadership. Only recently has the civil-rights movement raised the Negro's level of expectation and given him some sense of his political influence. Today the mayor's office is usually held by dedicated, knowledgeable men determined to face the reality of their cities' plight. With few exceptions, old-fashioned ward politics has disappeared from the cities and been replaced by honest, if not strong, political organizations. A professionalism has also grown up in urban affairs; city managers, highly trained social workers, and city planners give local governments a new coterie of experts.

Certainly the national government has filled an important role, and local governments cannot shun federal money and ideas and concern because of some lingering echoes about local autonomy. They must seek and welcome help from everywhere, and indeed they have been doing so for many years. The national government has a legitimate concern with the life of the city. The Department of Housing and Urban Development, the model cities program, and the new Department of Transportation are fresh and heartening signs of the national government's continuing interest in urban affairs and of its new understanding of the need for coordinated approaches. But the national government cannot deal effectively with every local government. Direct federal assistance has often resulted in confusion and waste motion at the local level. There is also the danger of massive mistakes if too much uniformity prevails from Boston to Santa Fe. No single government can work successfully with 18,000 municipalities and 3,043 counties, to say nothing of 18,323 special districts and some 34,000 school districts. The national government needs a go-between if its efforts are to be consistent with and are not to jeopardize the long-range goals of all local governments.

Many cities by-pass the states as much as possible in their

dealings with the national government, and most think they would like to do so. A former governor of an urban state told me:

The big-city administrators get to Washington the day after the legislation is passed and get their claims in. I call them super-cities. They can do the staff work and carry it out, whereas the rest of the cities aren't able to do it. . . . Maybe we ought to look at things as they are and recognize that the super-cities are going to keep on going to Washington. They are used to doing it and they are not going to change overnight. And furthermore, with their political strength . . . they will probably appeal over a governor's head anyway if they don't get the attention they think they should have. Maybe we have a two-level system of Federal aid—one that administers directly to these large cities and one that takes care of the rest of the state. . . .

We may be a "nation of cities" but not all cities are able to mount a campaign of the type St. Louis or Chicago can. They do not have the manpower, leadership, or political power. In fact, the special pleaders for direct city ties to Washington contend that more people live in large cities than actually do.

The 1960 population distribution by city size reveals that 48.3 per cent of the nation's total population lived in rural areas or in cities of under 50,000 people (which means approximately 15,000 families)—and that only 9.8 per cent lived in cities of over one million population. Of the more than 6,000 legally constituted cities in the nation, only five have a population of over one million, and only 50 have populations of over 250,000.[7]

The relationship between state and city governments must be effected in two aspects—with super-cities, and with the more numerous towns and smaller cities. The super-cities, with populations larger than those of some states, have and should have direct lines to Washington from their mayors.

In fact, an alert state administration will help in developing these lines. These cities need the direct federal help they are already receiving. Nonetheless super-cities do not cover enough land area or enclose enough people within their limits to justify their mayors' seeking federal aid without involving the states. They are surrounded by heavily populated suburban areas that will not be fairly or adequately served if federal assistance rests on no broader base than the demands of the big city halls. The states must be involved, not in a struggle with the super-cities, but as the leader concerned with all urban citizens. The cities need help from the state governments. Such help is their right. Small cities and towns need even more help from the states, and of different kinds. But saying this is not enough. The needs of urbanizing America are not defined by inventorying the needs of the cities and towns. The necessities are far more extensive, and are primarily and directly the responsibility of state government. My first recommendation calls upon the states to grasp the broad picture, beyond the city and the city-state relationship as they now exist. It is the state, not the city, that has the basic responsibility for urban America.

1. *The challenge of the urban areas must be accepted by the states, since only the state is in the position to bring order to urban growth. Each state should develop a forceful and competent department or agency for urban affairs.*

I do not believe the cities are developing in a healthy pattern. I believe we must find ways to discourage and avoid the unordered piling up of problems upon problems. That New York City will increase in population by any projection of past growth figures is terrifying. New Yorkers cannot say this. They cannot stop promoting, packing, building, squeezing, rising—it is a compulsion that also infects the chambers of commerce of Kansas City, Omaha, and Mobile in like degree. Growth, continued growth, bigger and bigger, is the creed of almost every city and town.

New York City, like a fat man, needs to change to a more healthful diet and take off weight under the doctor's orders and supervision. It doesn't need more industry. It needs less. It doesn't need to gain population in the next decade. It needs to lose population. And other cities, observing the obesity of New York and the bulging waistline of Los Angeles, need to change diets before high blood pressure and gout clobber their vitality. One of the first things the states can do is help and guide the cities to stop, look around, and start over.

The mayor of New York estimated that to rejuvenate the city would require $50 billion from the national government —a top-of-the-head guess, for there is no knowing. Nor, more to the point, is there any way to know what the cities would be a generation after we spent this vast mountain of money. Indeed, we will never have enough money to rejuvenate and re-rejuvenate the tangle of cities we are frantically building. To be sure, most of our cities are not already too large, but the super-cities are, and all cities have the wrong criteria for growth. All are, by creed, anxious to be too large.

Lewis Mumford spoke to the same Senate subcommittee which heard the predictions of the need for $50 billion dollars over the next ten years in New York City alone. He said:

Such a massive expenditure succeeded, we all know, in producing the atom bomb; and it has been applied with equal success in producing rockets, space satellites, supersonic jets, and similar instruments of physical conquest or destruction. I beg you to look more closely at what such a huge supply of capital with such large prospective profits would do. Not merely would [$50 billion as bait] skyrocket already inflated land values so that a disproportionate amount would go to property owners and real estate speculators; but even worse—it would invite greater megamachines to invade the building industry. . . . With the aid of their systems analyzers and computers, these high-powered organizations would design housing units even more prison-like in character than those we now have, and as unfit for permanent human habitation.

Not many mayors can be expected to call a halt to the growth-at-any-price which is the hallmark of municipal progress. If one did, there would not be available to him the means of directing a reasonable slowdown. Nor should one mayor act independently of the other communities, for likely he would stifle the remaining industry and population if his program were not a part of a larger concern for the cumulation of population, transportation, and jobs.

The steps are many a mayor can take to create a livable environment and a scope of employment advantageous to the city residents. But they are limited. He needs help beyond his authority and capacity. Even if help is generous, such as the coordinated plan and unrestricted money of the model-cities program, it is not enough. With all such help, the mayors still must run their separate races against doomsday, and there is no escaping the finality of its arrival if they are compelled to run alone.

The states cannot evade their duty. The national government has money, but the states have the legal authority to unite the cities in a joint and winning race. The city cannot solve its problems permanently unless its problem-solving devices reach out effectively to surrounding territory. They do not. Vast metropolitan governments have not been very successful, and complete annexation runs against the preferences of too many people to be presented as the final solution. Anchorage does not want to be a part of Louisville, perhaps for very valid reasons. The uniting, the consolidation of local governments, cannot be by legislative fiat. While annexation and consolidation have been neglected and are urgent requirements in some places, these approaches have their limitations. There is more territory than can be consolidated, and functions of government beyond city responsibilities are involved. Moreover, future growth will not confine itself to the consolidated boundaries no matter how extensively they might be drawn. The states, more so than either the national government or local governments, are in the position to guide the urbanization bursting upon this country.

Mayor John Lindsay has brought to his office a freshness and intelligence not surpassed in any American city. But beyond imaginative administration, New York City needs the assistance of national funds, and no matter how freely they might be handed out, it still needs help. New York City is the vortex of the Northeast urban whirlpool, and all interests flow in and out. But its authority stops and its capacity to influence fades rapidly at the city limits. The states hold the tools, even if many are rusty from disuse. As a matter of fact, there is not any other source of sufficient strength—not a band of mayors, not the national government—capable of saving the city from the city. The governors of Connecticut, New Jersey, and New York, on behalf of the people of New York City and supporting environs, should join together immediately and in a sense of urgency, to oil up the rusty tools and assume the duty of planning and carrying out the action needed to revitalize the New York City area. The Mayor of New York cannot do it alone, for the burdensome problems of his New York are only a part of the total problem of the total area of what is called New York. It is a dereliction to leave the health of the cities to fragmentary cures available from Washington.

All the states must assume the urban tasks—as landscaper, architect, traffic manager, builder, author, and visionary. The state, with possession of taxing, annexation, eminent domain, and zoning powers, the over-all view and supervisory position, can be more successful than any other government in designing and encouraging a proper use of the land that provides for present needs while protecting the future uses. It can preserve the open spaces while they are still open to be preserved. Whether it uses its power of eminent domain, or wise tax policies that favor dedication to open space, or the negotiated purchase of building rights, or other proposed means as the device for setting land aside, the overrunning of open land by urban sprawl must be contained. To me open space does not mean just city parks; it means unmanicured farms, forests and lakes, protected in perpetuity from housing subdivisions, factories, offices, warehouses, and apartments. A proper vision of such land use can be gained only from a view beyond the center city, and adequate will and strength can be found only beyond the city hall. The total power of accomplishment, it is true, must come from center and suburban city, combined with county and state government, and the national government. The ultimate legal authority resides in state government, and the way is wide open for leadership. Here is both the chance and the urgent duty for states to lead.

We will have committed an immensely costly error if we look at our urban problem as simply a matter of cleaning out and patching up. To be sure, it is all that, but it is vastly more. Transportation into cities cannot be limited to freeways and dingy commuter trains. Parking provisions and rapid, clean, and cheap transportation are not beyond our ingenuity. I have not conducted a traffic count, but every time I participate in the rush-hour traffic between Chicago's Loop and O'Hare I observe that the freeway automobile occupants do not average much more than the driver. There is not enough space for such transportation. Mass transportation is an obvious next step for the future of urban areas. Cities from Los Angeles to Dallas to Chicago are molding themselves to the freeway, and are fast reaching a saturation point. No city alone can put a handle on this problem because mass transit involves intercity cooperation, and will determine the growth patterns of areas around the cities, as well as the location of new towns and regional cluster cities. The states have sufficient overview. The states have the reach and the resources to make mass transportation work. It will take a freshness of view, but no call to duty is louder, and no opportunity for creative service by the urban states is more immediate.

The states can promote and encourage better housing, drawing together and filling in the gaps of numerous programs which have dehumanized whole landscapes, left slums and the makings of future slums in their wake, and neglected an entire wedge of the population not able to afford the profitable housing developments and not eligible or willing to live in public housing. The state can consolidate, zone, design, and channel the separated city clusters of the future. The national government does not have the legal authority or the instruments for carrying out action, and the cities do not have the position or outlook. The states have all these.

The cities need self-help and outside help. They need money. They need more than money, and we must come to the clear understanding that a city's vexations are only a part of the urban problem. The larger problem belongs to the states. The methods of the states will require a degree of intelligence and courage not yet exhibited, but there is no other full hope.

Surely there is a better fate for us than to continue to grow up and up. There is a cemetery in New Orleans, to me a bizarre place, where vaults are piled one on top of the other as the lower ones over the years sink deeper and deeper. Ever since a cabdriver first pointed it out and told me this story, I think of the American city as I pass this graveyard.

The urban challenge is the governor's challenge, and he should build the mechanism for bringing together all the urban services and programs offered by the various state departments and agencies. Except for a few, all states need a special department or agency for urban affairs. The governor cannot leave to the cities or to any others the central position, because only the state occupies the center. The governor must always take the initiative and assume the responsibility for working where the people are.

Why a new agency or department, especially when there is a cry to reduce the number of competing and pyramiding state agencies? First, the states need to redress the image of unconcern, of lack of interest in urban people and problems. The unapportioned legislature has given a rural tone to state activities. The establishment of a strong department of urban or community affairs is a positive signal to the local governments and the urban residents that a change has occurred. It is important that the states run up this flag, for the states will need widespread public support if they are to find a way to improve the cities. Second, there is a need for a focal point in the state, where somebody and some agency can take the interests of the urban areas to the highest level of state government decision. Local governments need a specific point in the state to turn to with complaints and grievances, as well as with their hopes. Certainly many agencies of the state are involved in the urban area problems, but local government is entitled to one place of support, and one champion before the legislative and executive branches.

Third, the federal programs require coordination, better communication, and technical competence; and the state can furnish these. Already Pennsylvania, New Jersey, Illinois, Washington, and about eight other states have established offices to work with urban needs and provide this essential help to cities and other local governments.

2. *The state, from its pivotal position in the federal system, must serve as coordinator, stimulator, representative,*

protector, and advisor for local governments in their relationships with the national government.

Most local governments do not have the personnel and professionalism required to draw together all federal programs designed to assist urban communities, and even if they could find enough people this would be needless and wasteful duplication.

The state governments already serve as the clearinghouse for information concerning many federal programs, and they are ideally located to provide an even more comprehensive service. Many already do. Not only can the state advise the local government, it can bring more than one city or community into a single project, when such cooperative effort is appropriate. It can recommend available programs and can initiate experimental approaches when demonstration grants would serve a useful purpose. It can prepare or assist in the preparation of proposals and applications. It can furnish qualified technicians to advise and guide.

The states can more nearly insist on coordination from the several national agencies when separate approaches prove inefficient. The states, out of their experience, can consult with the highest level of the national government in seeking improvement and consolidation of national efforts. That this has not been done is no excuse for refusing to try. Indeed the difficulties we have had in reaching the objectives we have set for ourselves, let alone those we have not got around to setting, demand some new approaches. A state working on behalf of its local governments will bring new strengths to the counties, cities, and towns and add effectiveness to the intent of Congress.

There are other ways a state urban-affairs agency could help local governments. It can encourage cooperative efforts for in-service training programs for local officials, for example in urban planning, slum removal, local government organization, recreation, and financial management. This might be done, as it is in some states, through a university, but wherever training is provided, the quality of local government improves.

States should also encourage and assist local and metropolitan planning agencies, and in some instances provide the service. Long-range planning—nothing more than organized and channeled forethought—is one of the most significant tools available as we attempt to shape the future. By planning, we avoid allowing crises to take us by surprise; we are able to anticipate them and plan our responses in a rational, thoughtful manner. The states, if they plan as they should, must include local planning, so technical assistance to the cities and towns serves a double purpose.

In transportation, for one example, we have moved from the day of the farm-to-market road into the day of mass travel within cities and between the cities and the suburbs. More roads beget more cars in a natural Parkinsonian way. The highway planners and builders, seeing more traffic, respond by projecting more highways. We are still thinking in terms of more highways and freeways for commuting purposes, although these reach the point of being both wasteful and inadequate. Families and homes are disrupted, neighborhoods are destroyed or isolated, and valuable land is eaten up and removed from the tax rolls as new freeways are laid down. The highways gain priority because the highway departments have long employed good planners. Their success is the best proof of our need for general planning. By 1970, if a rapid-transit system is not set up, it is estimated that Atlanta will need 120 expressway lanes radiating from downtown, along with a thirty-eight-lane central city connector. "Using these projections," one wag told me, "by the year 2000 all of Atlanta will be paved into one big freeway which should finally be adequate since it will obliterate the destination." The state can place all local plans in broad perspective, relating them and putting them in harmony with larger regional and state goals. The state must itself develop long-range master plans for all its activities, and in order to accomplish this in a comprehensive way, it needs to assist local government in making its own plans and projections.

Technical assistance to communities has long been furnished by the states—in such matters as recreation, health affairs, street construction, fire prevention, and civil defense, to name a few. Such assistance should be extended to the more difficult areas of public concern, such as housing and air pollution and the cleaning out of slums.

3. *The states must free local governments from the thicket of unworkable and out-of-date restraints on administrative structure, annexation, program activities, and personnel.*

The state legislature, where too much local authority is retained in the state capitol, should begin by granting local governments adequate legal powers, including liberalized annexation authority; rights for extraterritorial planning and zoning regulation; authority to set local salaries and personnel requirements and to contract or cooperate with other governments in providing services; and the power to transfer voluntarily functions from municipalities to counties and vice versa.

Local initiative is too often stifled by statutory or constitutional restrictions which impede necessary actions and encourage the proliferation of special districts. By 1962, there were 91,186 local governments in the United States, a whopping average of 1,824 per state! The problem is most serious in the most urban states. New York, California, Illinois, and Pennsylvania had more than 22 per cent of all governments, and these included special mosquito-control districts, sanitation districts, fire-protection districts, and even some cemetery districts, not to mention the general township, municipal, and county governments. These numbers are not necessarily bad and many of these separate governmental units serve well. But how many of them were established to circumvent outdated and restrictive state constitutions or statutory limits of various types?

Generally the states have not delegated enough home rule, and too many bills come before too many state legislatures setting the salaries of the local courthouse officials and the number of deputies authorized for the sheriff. This kind of local legislation is foolish for two reasons. It wastes the time of the state legislature, and it demeans the role of the local official.

Much innovative addition to the programs of the states, be they original programs or cooperative grant-in-aid ventures, can be gained from the enhancement of the county's role. They are arms of the states. While they and their counterparts present an almost endless variety of arrangement in the various states, presenting topics of book length in themselves, I have encompassed these governments in my thinking and in my comments about the states. I believe that in the states' renewed strength these governments will find new strengths. Several years ago the state of Connecticut took what was thought to be an innovative step in abolishing all county governments. But there are now some second thoughts on this. One official who had much to do with the bill told me, "We abolished county government here, and gave those functions to the cities and townships. Maybe what we should have done is abolish city government and kept county governments for a better overview and better coordination."

4. *The states must bring order out of local fiscal crisis.* Because the states set the ground rules for local government, they have explicit responsibility for seeing that their local units have the necessary revenue resources to carry out their responsibilities.

The states must free the local governments from unworkable restraints on their financial structure. Some tax sources are forbidden them and unrealistic ceilings are placed on their borrowing power. The results are self-evident: poor provision of services; excessive reliance on the regressive property tax; proliferation of special taxing districts; too much dependence on federal grants; and a series of missed opportunities.

The states must also move to consolidate, simplify, and strengthen the administration of property taxes. There are over 82,000 governmental units in the United States with property taxing powers. In Illinois alone, 5,388 governmental units have a taxing power. This can only lead to an overlapping, complicated, and often inequitable property tax structure. It also results in inadequate services. Only the states can change it.

The states, where the property tax laws lead to unworkable, unfair, or overly restrictive provisions, should revise the laws governing the tax base, limitations and exemptions, and administrative procedures. The states must determine the proper role of the property tax in the total state-local revenue system, and provide effective assistance and coordination in the administration of the tax. They should standardize assessment procedures for the sake of simplicity and as a safeguard against grossly unequal distribution of the property tax burden. Tax policies for local governments also are powerful devices for encouraging the protection of open spaces and the removal of substandard housing, by making these public policies somewhat profitable, but these are uses hardly explored by the states.

The problem is more than just removing the various and sometimes ingenious fiscal constraints on the local governments. The states must immediately provide more money to their local governments through increased grants and direct support of local government activities. The Advisory Commission on Intergovernmental Relations has long used the phrase that "the states must buy their way back into the urban areas." In a sense I agree with this, although state involvement must be much more than suggested by this simple phrase. But the message is clear—our problems are where the people are, and states must bring money and program to bear in the urban areas or find themselves permanently outside the federal-local axis, as the cities, however wrongly, step up their reliance on the national government for funds. The local governments must have access to the broader-based tax sources available to the states. In addition to increased support, the cities and other local governments could be helped by a lessening of restrictions in aid, a breaking down of partitions between programs, an approach to governmental problems based on planning and coordination. There is much evidence of need in local government for non-programmatic, general support for housekeeping functions— just as states feel they need unrestricted block grants from the national government. There is rarely enough money at the local level to carry on the governmental activities and services which must be provided. They must have general financial support from the states. In effect, the states could create a plan of support of local activities for those communities interested in better planning and coordination of effort. Such grants would help in bringing the disparate government units together, getting them around the table working with each other, setting common goals and choosing priorities, policies, and programs.

In urban affairs, the master concern is to make America more livable. It is not a battle for states' rights, local autonomy, or increased national power. The problems of the cities are the problems of the state, and they cannot be avoided. No member of the legislature is simply a delegate from his district. He is a part of a major branch of government in the federal system. All of his state, rural and urban, must be his concern, or the federal system will readjust to exclude him. We are talking not of buildings and traffic and walks through a park; we are talking of the quality of American life and the world in which we live. In an age when we move about in the heavens, surely we can summon our energy and intelligence to the task of a more civilized home for man. No governor can afford not to take his state where the people live.

1. "States Losing by Default," *The Atlanta Constitution*, March 31, 1967.
2. James A. Maxwell, *Financing State and Local Governments*, (Washington: The Brookings Institution, 1965), p. 75 and U.S., Bureau of the Census, *Governmental Finances in 1964–1965*, (Washington: U.S. Government Printing Office, 1966), p. 31.
3. *Ibid.*, p. 77.
4. Paul N. Ylvisaker, *Intergovernmental Relations at the Grass Roots: A Study of Blue Earth County, Minnesota, to 1946*, (Minneapolis: University of Minnesota Press, 1956), pp. 134–135.
5. Morton Grodzins, *The American System, A New View of Government in the United States*, edited by Daniel J. Elazar, (Chicago: Rand McNally & Company, 1966), pp. 171–172.
6. *Ibid.*, pp. 157–167, *passim*.
7. Daniel J. Elazar, "Are We a Nation of Cities?," *Public Interest*, No. 4, (Summer, 1966), p. 43.

CHAPTER XIV

Be Proud to Pay State Taxes

It is odd, but the national government seldom receives the severe rebuke voters often voice toward the states. People are much more forbearing and indulgent toward their national government than toward their states. It has become almost commonplace to talk of "tax-loss" governors. This term does not mean that the governor lost any tax, or that the revenue picture was not solid. It means that he had the nerve to call for a tax increase and for this reason was defeated at the next election. Who has heard of a "tax-loss" congressman? The national government raises and lowers taxes with impunity, and certainly imposes the heaviest, although maybe not the most irritating, tax. Seldom, however, is a congressman even questioned about it, much less taken to task.

Another oddity, in my observation, is that the voters most outspoken against centralization are exactly those who most vocally condemn all state taxes. These objectors are totally inconsistent. The states must not become fiscal wards of the national government unless we are content to let the national government make most of the decisions. The primary means for keeping the federal system from becoming top-heavy is to keep the states financially vital.

Perhaps the fact that the states are "closer to the people" makes them vulnerable. The states are scolded for any expenditure for something new. In one state too wide to drive across in a day, the legislature had authorized the purchase

of a small airplane to ferry industrial prospects and for other
governmental use. The jangle against the airplane rose and
fell with lunar regularity. One week, when the matter was
the subject of current criticism, a governor's aide recalls, a
U.S. cabinet officer and two federal agency heads flew to
the state capital in a jet with a capacity of at least twenty-five
passengers. Later in the same week an assistant secretary
with a staff of six flew in a four-engine plane to two cities
in the state. Not a word was said about the federal planes.
Nor should there have been. The cabinet member was on
an urgent mission for the President of the United States. The
assistant secretary was on a regional tour of conferences
with a schedule which made any other kind of travel difficult.
In any event, it is not the purpose here to comment on the
validity of the air travel by the national representatives. The
point is that such silly discrimination on the part of the citizen has been one reason the states have felt backward. It is
hard to compete vigorously when the home crowd is throw-
ing rotten vegetables at the home team.

In 1966, Governor William H. Avery of Kansas was defeated. A conservative congressman, he had acted in a completely consistent manner when, as governor, he boldly
insisted on new state taxes for education. No doubt other
factors helped bring about his defeat, but the fact remains
that he became another governor who had the nerve to "impose" new taxes, and lost. Robert Smylie, as governor of
Idaho, met the same fate.

Finally, I was able to convince the Republican legislators, but
even then not the party hierarchy, that the consequences of a bold
new departure [for a new revenue structure] would be less dangerous politically than a do-nothing record. It is ironical that on
that issue I was shot down, but that the party prospered at the
polls.[1]

But encouraging signs come from Massachusetts, Michigan, New Jersey, Maryland, and California. Governor Volpe put through the Massachusetts legislature a 3 per cent sales tax and was overwhelmingly re-elected at the same time that the voters approved his tax by a margin of five to one. Governor Romney of Michigan was re-elected by a comfortable margin despite the fact that he insisted more taxes were needed to provide for the state's needs. In 1965, Governor Richard Hughes of New Jersey made it plain throughout his campaign that he would fight for a broad-based tax. He called for and delivered a 3 per cent sales tax after narrowly losing an income tax. In California, Governor Ronald Reagan wrestled with his state's fiscal problems, and asked the legislature for tax reform and tax increases which would bring in nearly one billion dollars per year for California, a large portion of it for property tax relief, yet the largest request for a state tax increase in history.

In 1967, Maryland, under leadership of Governor Spiro T. Agnew, "enacted a wholesale reform of its fiscal structure that will stand as a model of responsibility and fiscal soundness for a long time to come." [2] A graduated income tax replaced a flat-rate income tax; capital gains were taxable for the first time; a mandatory "piggyback" local income tax from 20 to 50 per cent of the state tax replaced three county income taxes and the Baltimore city payroll tax; and a new system of state grants-in-aid was established to aid the poorest counties and the city of Baltimore. "The new grants and the piggyback local taxes will prevent a property tax increase of as much as 60 cents per $100 assessed valuation in the counties and Baltimore City." [3] The new state income tax structure will increase state revenue by an estimated 74 per cent and will shift the tax burden from people with low incomes to those with high incomes. Each of these states might be classified as an urban state, with major urban concentrations within their boundaries. The difficulties of city life are more and more being dumped into the laps of the governors. And now with reapportionment, their legislatures are urban-suburban in outlook and in partnership with the governors are forecfully bringing the states' fiscal resources to bear on their urban problems.

Taxes, so unpleasant and so politically hazardous, constitute the red corpuscles of government. I make no case for new taxes as such. A state administration should be under strong moral compulsion to stay within its revenues, and to prevent wasteful spending at every turn. The case to be made is for an adequate tax program. It is a necessity. A state which is not investing in its own future is not going to have a bright one. The educational needs and possibilities are exciting and expanding. The needs people create as they congregate in urban areas stagger us as we talk not of millions of dollars, but of billions for city center renewal and revitalization and for proper development of surrounding metropolitan areas. A mental-health officer in Minnesota summed it up: "Money isn't the only problem. But it's so far ahead of number two, it's the one we've got to talk about." Any state content to remain in old ruts in order to practice false economy is not going to see its people earn the money and make the progress citizens of other states are making. Neither is it doing much to strengthen its position or its future as a worthwhile part of the federal system.

But what is an adequate tax program? Simply put, an adequate tax program is one which provides the funds necessary for handling competently the problems of the state and its people. Within this broad definition, a state should, of course, try to construct as equitable and progressive a tax program as possible. These principles leave a lot of leeway.

Raising enough state funds for the future will not be the easiest task facing state leaders. Joseph A. Pechman of the Brookings Institution projected the following in 1965:

Suppose gross national product grows at 5 per cent per annum and state-local receipts (including federal grants) keep pace with this growth. On these assumptions, state-local receipts would reach about $88 billion by 1970. But if needed state-local expenditures grow at 7 per cent per annum—which seems conservative in the light of past experience—they would reach $103 billion by 1970, leaving a gap of about $15 billion.[4]

A consultant to the Committee for Economic Development estimated in 1965 that the gap would be $10 billion by 1970.[5] The State-Local Finances Project at George Washington University sees little or no gap at the turn of the next decade —but this result depends on nearly one-fifth of the estimated $108 billion of state-local expenditures coming from federal grants-in-aid.[6]

Recently two reports have been issued which are even more sanguine. According to a new study by the Committee on Economic Development, "These calculations suggest that through 1975, state and local governments can secure the funds to finance expansions in expenditures incorporating significant improvements in scope and quality without increases in tax rates or broadening of the tax base."[7] The Tax Foundation has also indicated that "aggregate general revenues will grow more rapidly than spending in the decade ahead, without an increase in over-all tax rates. . . . For most state and local units, the financial outlook is much better than is generally realized."[8]

It is true that this world of statistics doesn't seem to conform to the world of unmet needs. Why have New York, California, New Jersey, Massachusetts, and Michigan been forced to take such giant steps to raise funds at the time these reports were being issued? And these large urban states are not alone.

Over the 1963–65 biennium, more than three-fourths of the states had enacted revenue-raising legislation—a larger number than in any of the three preceding bienniums. . . . Among the states raising tax rates, there were relatively few in which only marginal amounts of additional revenue were sufficient to balance budgets. . . . The record volume of revenue legislation in 1965 reflected an all-time high in expenditures proposed for the next two years.[9]

Walter Heller warns, "Before anyone reaches this complacent conclusion [that revenues will be sufficient for the needs in state and local governments], let him knock on any fiscal door or scratch any fiscal surface at the state or local level." [10]

From a combination of the reports I find an encouraging note. It may very well be, as Walter Heller says, that if you probe the reality you will discover tax pressures in every state and locality. There is a shortage of revenues to accomplish what most legislators and governors think should be done. But this pressure relates to today, and out of the reports I draw the encouragement that the bases of state taxation are improving, and that increased incomes will provide some states the needed money without increased tax rates. Increases in revenues will not be adequate in every state, but the states are not bankrupt. In general, the sources are healthy and are constantly growing. The states cannot do without the financial assistance from the national government, because our tax patterns have made this a fact of American government. They can, however, come closer to handling their fiscal requirements if they will now go about the job of intelligently shaping their own tax programs. If they will do their home duty, as many are doing already, the states need not become as dependent on the Federal treasury as some fear. Washington Governor Daniel J. Evans reminded us in an interview of what many are slow to confess: "The states can do more and are not really as poor as they claim to be." The states cannot expect to carry on all needed programs without federal grants-in-aid, as I have already suggested, but they can get on with their responsibilities without waiting at the gate for some kind of "revenue sharing without strings" which will not arrive while most present governors are still in office.

True, this kind of revenue sharing has appeal, as Leon H. Keyserling notes:

This entire question of revenue-sharing arises because our economic growth will, within a few years, yield large increases in Federal income, even at existing tax rates. I estimate that during the decade ahead about $550 billion *more* in Federal taxes would be collected at an optimum growth rate.[11]

What to do with this sizable increase bothers economists. What will it do to the total economy to have this much additional tax drawn off? How should it be reduced or redistributed? Would commensurate tax cuts and lessening of public expenditures slow the private sector of the economy? Would applying the surplus to the national debt likewise slow the economy? Should it be channeled back through the states? There does appear to be a consensus on one point: increased national funds will be available for the needs of the country, unless we engage in a widespread war. If this is true, some tax sharing by relatively unrestricted transfers to the states of a percentage of the personal income tax revenues is a probability in the future.

Our unmet agenda is staggering: air pollution, water pollution, mass and rapid transit, urban and rural education, special education, housing, poverty, police and fire protection, mental health, conservation, recreation, and urban renewal, to name a few. And the demand to do something about each of these items is increasing, not remaining stable or declining.

The states are responding to the agenda with their largest budgets in history and with major increases in taxes to support them. Because these funds are not enough, there is an increasing call by the states and the cities for a share of the federal funds obtained through the federal income tax. It is understandable that longing eyes should be cast on this source of additional funds. This is the most progressive tax, the fastest growing of major taxes, the easiest to collect. That state and local leaders feel it would be a wise national tax policy for all three levels to share in these collections is not surprising. That there will be sharing in the costs of programs is not to be doubted; the proposition now being put is of deeper significance.

The present emerging debate is over whether these funds should be with or without strings. Should they come to state and local governments for specific purposes, as in the past, or should they come to be spent as the state and local governments see best—perhaps within certain broad limits? This adds up to the choice on one side of an extension and expansion of categorical grant-in-aid programs and, on the other, the plan advanced by Walter Heller while he was chairman of the President's Council of Economic Advisors. The essence of the suggestion is that a certain percentage of federal personal income tax collections be transferred to the states for general-purpose use with very few limitations as to the category in which the funds must be spent. In any event there are at present unusual military expenditures, so my own prediction is that the final decision on this question will be postponed for several years.

There is a middle ground which the states should cultivate during these several years. It suggests positive and constructive action by all participants in our federal system and not the "something for nothing" attitude of some of those who have picked up the Heller plan.

First, I believe the states must get their tax houses in order.

They can do so through the determination of each state to look at its taxes objectively and to shape a fair tax program that assures adequate revenues. Self-reliance of this kind is essential to self-respect and to authenticate the faith that states do have a significant role, as well as the intent and the capacity to carry it out. They cannot just give up and look for a grant-in-aid or wait and hope for a block grant or a tax-sharing plan of some sort. Congressional leaders and citizens are not going to look on states with much favor if their only pose is with the hand extended, palm up. Furthermore, Congress will surely insist on some minimum tax effort, such as a designated ratio between the tax dollar collected by the state and the gross personal income within the state. Possibly Congress would insist on some basic design or structure of state taxation as a condition for receiving transfers of unrestricted payments. Far better it is that the states put their own tax programs in order, rather than be forced to do so.

I have recorded some examples of state fiscal responsibility, where political leaders have chosen the hard way of meeting public trust head on by increasing state taxes. Yet there are still seven states without a broad-based general sales tax,[12] thirteen states without an individual income tax,[13] and eleven states without a corporate income tax.[14] Several of the states that do have these taxes limit their effectiveness as revenue producers by exemptions of various types. I am not advocating that all states have the same tax structure, for I believe strongly in the diversity which is at the base of our federal system and in the right of each state to determine its own best tax structure. Each state must approach its tax structures from where it sits and on the basis of what has been done in the past. Those states without the personal income tax must give consideration to adopting it, and those with an ineffective income tax should consider strengthening it. I would suggest that the states also examine all the other obvious tax sources they do not now employ, be they corporate income, general sales, or whatever, as well as examining the effective rates, the exemptions, and the loopholes of the taxes they do levy. In some instances they may find parts of their program, perhaps local property taxes, which are unduly burdensome and merit tax relief, but they will certainly find more unused and underused tax sources. This is not a popular topic—taxes—but it is the one basic answer to the loss of authority and decision to the national government.

A Missouri legislator added another bit of advice: "If you want to do the states a favor, suggest they pass a withholding tax. It's the best thing we ever did. We caught the people we missed who work in our state but live across the line. And because the people didn't have to pay all the tax in one bite, the opposition to all taxes melted considerably." The spirit of this first recommendation is for the states, if they really have pride in being states, to do all that they can do before turning elsewhere.

To wait for every state to make the necessary reforms before Congress acts on general grants or tax sharing would penalize those states that are putting their tax houses in order and still need additional funds. There is a limited way the Congress can aid the overburdened state that is making a conscientious effort, and, at the same time, entice other states to utilize the most progressive and productive of taxes, the income tax. It is the most productive because it taps an ever-increasing commodity and grows rapidly as our country and economy grow. This suggests another recommendation.

Second, I believe that Congress should enact the so-called income tax-credit plan. In this belief, I agree with the recommendation of the Advisory Commission on Intergovernmental Relations that federal income taxpayers be allowed to claim a substantial percentage of their state income tax payments as a credit against their federal income tax liability.[15]

This credit would be available to all taxpayers who pay a state income tax, and would be subtracted from the amount of federal income tax otherwise paid. This simply means that if the income tax due the federal government was $1,200 and the income tax paid the state government was $200, the taxpayer would owe the federal government only $1,000. It is not likely the credit would be for 100 per cent, but if it were 50 per cent, the taxpayer would owe $1,100 to the federal government. It is possible that an equitable schedule would be sought by Congress which would make more certain that the taxes credited would go to the states. The purpose of this tax credit is to put money in the state treasury which otherwise would be paid to the national government. It would behoove states, where necessary, to increase their rates to take up the slack as to do so would not cost the taxpayer any more. This is not to be viewed as tax relief; that can be afforded more simply. This is a way of transferring some of the national tax collection to the states. It is just a matter of which government gets the revenue. For those states without an income tax, this would be an inducement, but not a requirement, to levy such a tax. This is a clear and clean way of putting the money where it is needed.

If in the future some variation of the Heller plan may be adopted, then it is fair that in the beginning the state income tax situation be somewhat consistent. Adopting the tax credit plan as the first step will go a long way toward developing such consistency. It will not require conformity to any model state tax plan, but it will provide some degree of uniformity and make more equitable future distribution of federal collections. The taxpayer would pay no more. No one can complain except the states without an income tax, and they cannot complain much if they are among those who hope to share in revenue from the income tax levied by and in the name of the national government. If these states are willing to accept an income tax indirectly through a tax-sharing plan, it is reasonable for them to get the first part of the income tax in their own name. Before we go to something like a Heller plan, each state should have a relatively equal tax burden of its own. Otherwise, states would continue to compete for the prize for being the lowest income tax state, and this competition is part of the reason for a turn to the Heller proposal anyhow.

Third, the federal government must relax its stringent and multiple requirements for the many grant-in-aid programs, and take steps to consolidate them into fewer, broader grants.

This suggestion, if carried out, may illustrate the usefulness and feasibility of block grants and revenue sharing, and certainly will alleviate some tax pressures the states face. It will give them more leeway with their existing state funds and national grants-in-aid. The 89th Congress has opened the door for this with "The Comprehensive Health Planning and Public Health Services Amendments" of 1966. These amendments allow the states to work on a number of health problems in total rather than segment by segment. A direct result will be not only more flexibility in allocation of priorities and funds, but more responsibility stimulated at the state and local levels in planning and implementing these programs. If we truly believe our state and local governments are partners in the system rather than administrators, then this participation afforded by block grants is a major step which will reinforce and, in some cases, introduce the partnership.

The grant-in-aid is primarily, it has been argued, for the purpose of creating new effort and emphasis where Congress believes it should be created. In time, maybe in some instances no more than five years, the intent of the emphasis should have been accomplished, and the aid funds can be shifted to general support. One method for doing this is by block grants in a broad field of governmental responsibility, such as the shift in the health grants. Another way is by a general sharing of the national income tax revenues.

Fourth, once the grants are more comprehensive than categorical and more open than restricted, after a tax credit act has been established, and the states have their fiscal houses in order, *Congress should construct a broad tax-*

sharing program based on the federal income tax revenues. This final step is the Heller plan, or at least a variation. Under this proposal, a certain percentage of the federal income tax revenues, probably around one or two per cent, would be earmarked each year for distribution to the states. A portion of the money would be reserved solely for the poorer states, with the rest being distributed on a population basis. Returning the funds in this way would achieve a moderate redistribution of the nation's wealth, aiding those states which have honestly reached their taxing capacity, yet, because of certain economic conditions, are in greater need than others. The grant programs achieve this redistribution to a degree, but in a rather haphazard manner. The income tax-credit plan does not, but it has other advantages.

These funds could be used by the state and local governments in many diverse ways, just as any other state funds. If we look to revenue sharing as a fourth step, we do away with many of the arguments and fears of unrestrained use, reduction of state contributions, or failure to continue federal programs. These funds become additional general revenue to the states, subject to the usual procedures of state appropriations. I would not contemplate that adoption of a revenue sharing plan would eliminate the grant approach. Congress needs and would retain this method of directing nationwide effort.

There are many persuasive reasons for adopting this plan as a means of partial support of government in states and cities. It will increase our chances of success and the impact of some of our major programs of government—education, health, welfare, employment, prisons, natural resources, and recreation. These shared funds will beef up the administrative side of our state and local governments. The former Commissioner of Administration of Minnesota, Ray Lappegaard, makes the perceptive argument: ". . . one of the advantages of the Heller plan is that grants without any designation which are returned to the states, would be used for enlarging the role of the state government and not . . . for enlarging the role of the federal government." [16] The major purpose is indeed to work at the needs of America while protecting and strengthening the federal system.

The mayors look at the tax sharing plan both eagerly and with trembling. They are eager for the money but fear letting the states get their hands on it. The plan of tax sharing must ensure that our local governments receive the benefits. The states should be developing their attention to the cities long before Congress is ready to enact revenue sharing, and should have prepared the way for major participation by local governments.

I only recommend a broad-based tax sharing program as a final item after the first three recommendations have been achieved. All four steps are necessary to assure the fiscal capacity of our states and localities to serve the needs of people while maintaining the integrity of our federal system. Congress has a responsibility for achieving this balance, but the states have the first responsibility. In short, the states, before asking for an unrestricted part of the national tax collections, must have the character to do the taxing they are entitled, expected, and competent to do. How else can they say they should survive as governments? If the people do not want the states to be effective taxing governments, then they do not really want them to be governments.

1. Letter from Robert F. Smylie, former Governor of Idaho, February 1, 1967.
2. Joesph Pechman, "Fiscal Reform in Maryland," *Nation's Cities*, (April, 1967), p. 14.
3. *Ibid.*, p. 51.
4. Joseph A. Pechman, "Financing State and Local Government," *Proceedings of a Symposium on Federal Taxation*, (New York: American Bankers Association, 1965), p. 76.

5. Dick Netzer, "State-Local Finance in the Next Decade," unpublished manuscript for the Committee for Economic Development, (Washington: August, 1965), as reported in Walter Heller, *New Dimensions of Political Economy*, (Cambridge: Harvard University Press, 1966), p. 133.

6. Selma J. Mushkin and Robert F. Adams, "Emerging Patterns of Federalism," *National Tax Journal*, Vol. XIX, (September, 1966), p. 237.

7. *A Fiscal Program for a Better Balanced Federalism*, (Washington: Committee for Economic Development, 1967), p. 24.

8. *Fiscal Outlook for State and Local Government to 1975*, Government Finance Brief No. 7, (New York: The Tax Foundation Inc., 1966), p. 1.

9. Leon Rothenberg, "Recent Trends in State Taxation," *Book of the States, 1966–1967*, (Chicago: The Council of State Governments, 1966), p. 198.

10. Walter Heller, *op. cit.*, p. 133.

11. Leon H. Keyserling, "Sharing Revenue with the States," *The New Republic*, March 25, 1967, p. 15.

12. Those states without a broad-based general sales tax are: Alaska, Delaware, Minnesota, Montana, New Hampshire, Oregon, Vermont. *Book of the States, 1966–1967*, pp. 212–213.

13. Those states without an individual income tax are: Connecticut, Florida, Illinois, Maine, Michigan, Nevada, Ohio, Pennsylvania, Rhode Island, South Dakota, Texas, Washington, Wyoming. *Ibid.*, pp. 210–211.

14. Those states without a corporate income tax are: Florida, Illinois, Maine, Michigan, Nevada, New Hampshire, Ohio, Texas, Washington, West Virginia, Wyoming. *Ibid.*

15. U.S., The Advisory Commission on Intergovernmental Relations, *Federal-State Coordinating of Personal Income Taxes*, Report A-27, (Washington: U.S. Government Printing Office, 1965), pp. 15–19, 111–122.

16. Letter from Ray Lappegaard, Commissioner of Administration, State of Minnesota, May 13, 1966.

CHAPTER XV

Take It from the Top

Federal programs are uncoordinated, leading to overlapping, duplication, triplication, conflicting goals, cross purposes, lack of consistency, and loss of direction.

Congress enacts too many narrow, categorical grant programs with stringent guidelines, unnecessary requirements, and burdensome reporting procedures. These lead to waste motion and ineffective administration, weakening the capacities of state and local governments.

Governors and mayors are not consulted in planning legislation and not kept informed by federal officials on matters of concern to both.

These are the frequent complaints. The states can do very little to remove the causes of these complaints. Corrective action, if any, is up to the national government.

Since the depression, and particularly over the last ten years, the rising tide of new and expanded government activity has made obsolete the notion of clearly defined levels of government with clearly defined powers, and has introduced the principle of shared responsibilities. This shift does not represent a change in the basic structure of our federal system. It represents only a new consciousness of the constitutionally established principles of our system, and a new recognition that the system can adjust to the accelerating velocity of life.

It has become evident that there are difficulties in this system of shared responsibilities, but the difficulties arise not from the system itself, but from the manner in which we adapt and use the processes of the system. Our energies, so often dissipated in voluptuous reminiscence of simpler days, are better spent in seeking to refine those processes through which the system works. Our chore is to eliminate the factors which cause confusion and remove the features that weaken the capacity of any government—especially state and local— to meet its responsibilities. For

shared power is the key to the miracle of effective democratic government of a vast and diverse country. . . . State and local governments are increasing their activities more rapidly than the domestic sector of the federal government. Their load will continue to grow, and their capacity to meet it must be strengthened.[1]

Under the aegis of every President since Franklin D. Roosevelt, with a particular flurry of activity under Eisenhower, a variety of commissions, organizations, officials, and individuals have recommended improved ways of arranging and operating our intergovernmental activities. Many of the studies and reports were excellent and contain suggestions that are still relevant.[2] There were attempts to carry out some of the recommendations, but the attempts lacked vigor and the over-all result of most of the activity was limited. But the failures are instructive to those whose efforts continue today.

President Eisenhower was dedicated to the maintenance of "the constitutional relationship between the federal and state Governments."[3] A number of sorties were conducted during his administration. The most notable was the so-called Kestnbaum Commission Report, more formally *The Final Report of the Commission on Intergovernmental Relations.*[4] This commission, set up by Congress in 1953, conducted a highly creditable study of the federal-state relationship. It was exhaustive and comprehensive. The commission of twenty-five members with a professional staff of forty issued fifteen studies or publications in addition to its final report made in 1955. The following, it seems to me, is the heart of the report:

The maintenance of a healthy federal system has two aspects. The states must be alert to meet the legitimate needs of their citizens, lest more and more of the business of government fall upon the national government. At the same time, the national government must refrain from taking over activities that the states and their subdivisions are performing with reasonable competence, lest the vitality of state and local institutions be undermined.[5]

Seven members entered a footnote, one of several, indicating a variation of opinion:

It is a matter of regret that the Supreme Court of the United States in sustaining legislation designed to alleviate the effects of the depression of the 1930s has weakened the constitutional concept that the national government is one of delegated and enumerated powers and that "the powers not delegated to the United States by the Constitution, nor prohibited to it by the States, are reserved to the States respectively, or to the people." These decisions have fundamentally altered the balance of power designed by the architects of the Constitution.[6]

Senator Wayne Morse held an opposing point of view and filed a dissent to the entire report. "It is because I do not think that the report of the commission gives due emphasis to the rights and jurisdiction of federal sovereignty that I file this dissent."[7]

The study, and the fact that there was a study, brought new attention to the difficulties caused by the sporadic development of federal programs. It prompted new concern and additional interest in readjusting the federal-state relationship. President Eisenhower brought Howard Pyle, former governor of Arizona, to Washington as deputy assistant for intergovernmental relations. He also established Meyer Kestnbaum, who had been chairman of the commission, in the White House with instructions to follow up on the work of the commission.

It is probably not unfair to say that very few important changes were carried through. Such are the obstacles. The work stands today, however, as a relevant if not final guide for those who seek, in the words of the preface to the *Report,* to improve the "role of the federal Government in relation to the States and their political subdivisions." [8]

President Eisenhower also stirred up enough interest to set up what was called the Joint Federal-State Action Committee. It consisted of nine governors and seven top officials of the national government. This committee didn't live up to its name. If it recommended action, it was at very best only modest action.

The committee recommended that the states assume a greater share of the responsibility for the health and safety regulation of nonmilitary applications of atomic energy. The Atomic Energy Commission has made a genuine effort to get states to assume such duties; seventeen have.[9] It also recommended that each state create an agency to handle urban and housing problems. A number have.[10]

The principal recommendation appears to have been a call on the national government to get out and leave to the states three activities: vocational education, waste treatment, and disaster relief. To finance, or help finance, these additional burdens, the Congress was to relinquish for taxation by the states part of the national tax on local telephone service.[11] Nothing was ever done about either of these.

Actually, for all the work of the Federal-State Action Committee at the time, these recommendations strike the reader today as rather puny assaults on the problem. More fundamentally, they were not soundly based on the concept of shared responsibilities, a procedure even then already firmly embedded, even if not fully comprehended.

There are several continuing bodies that constantly evaluate our federal system and suggest ways in which intergovernmental relations can be enhanced. The U.S. House of Representatives has a Subcommittee on Intergovernmental

Relations, headed by Congressman L. H. Fountain. This sub-committee has carried on much significant inquiry and re-search under the mandate of the Legislative Reorganization Act of 1946, charging both the Senate and the House Com-mittees on Government Operations (then called the Commit-tees on Expenditures in the Executive Departments) to study "intergovernmental relationships between the United States and the States and municipalities."

The Senate subcommittee in the same area is headed by Senator Edmund S. Muskie, a former governor of Maine who did not let the assumption of a Senate seat dim his memories of the difficulties often imposed on the states. For several years he has proposed legislation which would bring the national government to more careful consideration of intergovernmental relations, and would develop means for coordination of the heretofore uncoordinated efforts.

Another official body of the national government of con-tinuing significance is the Advisory Commission on Inter-governmental Relations. The commission, first established as a permanent body by Congress in 1959, includes representa-tives of federal, state, and local governments. Its purposes are to provide a forum for the discussion and improvement of grant-in-aid programs; to make technical assistance avail-able to the executive and legislative branches of the federal government; to encourage study of intergovernmental rela-tions; to recommend within the framework of the Constitu-tion the most desirable allocation of functions among the levels of government; and to seek ways to coordinate and sim-plify tax laws in order to achieve a more orderly and less competitive fiscal relationship among the governments.

Throughout its existence, the ACIR reports have been among the best in the intergovernmental field.[12] Their pub-lished recommendations to both the federal government and the states have been forward-looking and useful in giving a progressive program to the proponents of a better inter-governmental system.

In the private sector, the Committee for Economic Development has issued perceptive and constructive reports, covering the need for reform at all levels as well as specific recommendations for improvement.[18]

I could carry forward here the many excellent recommendations to improve federal-state relationships put forth in the numerous reports and studies of the past twenty years or so. My approach will be more general, on the premise that we need first to change the climate before we can use all the recommendations.

The first step in improving the federal-state-local system is the internal improvement of state government. No one can deny that. In fact, this book is mostly about that necessity and how the people can be of influence in accomplishing it. But that is not enough. There must also be both a restraint and a willingness to change on the part of the leaders of the national government. They cannot leave the commitment to federalism to those in state and local government alone. The commitment rests just as heavily with those working in national government, and perhaps more heavily. They own most of the precision tools, so much of the burden of refining and reshaping the relationship must be borne by those in Washington.

What we need right now is a commitment to several broad *central approaches* that the public can watch. From the point of view of Washington, and what might be done there, it seems to me that it would be useful for the national government to adopt five central approaches. There is no finality to these. This is not all that needs to be done. But if these approaches are firmly set and not evaded, by-passed, or sabotaged, their implementation, expansion, and detailed refinement would naturally flow from the advancing experience.

First, we need a presidential understanding that the federal system is now being shaped by the winds of hazard, that the national bureaucracy is inclined to random procedures that weaken the capacity of state government, and that

*only the White House can be effective in bringing order and
balance to the federal system.*

We need a White House understanding that action must
be of a new dimension, that repetition of the past efforts
will in all probability have the same results. Only the President has the position and authority to insist on the necessary
changes. The rock of bureaucratic resistance is too big for
anyone else to move.

I think the commitment is present with President Johnson.
He expressed his understanding in his State of the Union
message on January 10, 1967:

Federal energy is essential. But it is not enough. Only a total
working partnership among federal, state, and local governments
can succeed. The test of that partnership will be the concern of
each public organization, each private institution, and each responsible citizen.

Each state, county, and city needs to examine its capacity for
government in today's world. Some will need to reorganize and
reshape their methods of administration—as we are doing. Others
will need to revise their constitutions and their laws to bring
them up to date—as we are doing. Above all, we must find ways
in which multitudes of small jurisdictions can be brought together
more efficiently.

In commenting on the speech, James Reston said:

. . . the President is engaged in a number of remarkable experiments. . . . He is reaching out to the governors and mayors of
America for a new political, social, and economic partnership
within the nation. . . . He is not using Federal funds to impose
federal control over the states and cities . . . but to create new
partnerships between Washington and the state capitals and the
cities. . . .[14]

The "working partnership" the President proposes will not
be accomplished easily. Weak action will not accomplish
the purpose. Good words alone will have no lasting effect.

It is obvious that President Eisenhower was genuinely disturbed by the increase of centralization, and concerned about the future of our federalism. That his efforts were not strong enough is now a matter of history. Whether the President can translate his commitment to action, and whether he will be thwarted by the resistance which discouraged the Roosevelt and Truman starts and repelled the Eisenhower action are the remaining questions. In any event, the White House commitment to this first principle will be necessary after the present occupant is no longer there. The President must have an abiding personal interest in the proposition, and must transmit this interest to the officials in the national government in a number of ways, but always with presidential clarity and certainty and insistence. The strengthening of our federal system, and even its preservation, may very well be the most important domestic task for the President. As important as problem solving is, future problem solving depends on what we do to the federal-state-local relationship in the process.

Even with the President's commitment and authority, we lack a clearly defined goal. We favor creative federalism, but what is it? We favor a smoother partnership, but what should be the role of each partner in a creative federal system? We need better definition of what we hope to do.

Second, a national goal should be enunciated, setting forth the determination to strengthen the federal system.

After some two hundred years of life as a dynamic society with a dynamic government, we need to declare our purpose to protect our federal system from jarring loose at the seams. The precise words of the proposed declaration are not important. The essential thing is to have a policy statement to guide the direction of governmental action. A policy statement will help fix our concept of shared responsibilities as they become more and more a fixed pattern in American government. The danger is that one government may begin to dominate most of the action to the exclusion or weakening of the other governments. We avoid this danger if we plot our directions in advance. The President may desire to make a statement of policy as he forms his own lines for White House activity. Or Congress may make a policy statement in a resolution, or as part of an act relating to some federal-state-local relationship. Or the statement may appear in other forms. The cardinal need, it seems to me, is that the statement of purpose or goal be formulated by the national government from a position of political strength, in fresh and pertinent terms relevant to intergovernmental relationships as they have now developed.

Such a policy statement should include the following elements:

Effective state government is essential to the healthy development of the United States of America.

It is the continuing purpose of the national government, directly and indirectly, to improve the effectiveness of state governments, recognizing that they must have freedom to innovate and strength to resist.

National programs of assistance and involvement should not be allowed to weaken the states by circumvention, domination or regimentation, in either policy shaping or administration; rather it should be the national purpose to design national programs so as to promote the continual renewal of state and local governments in their capacity to solve problems and serve the communities of the nation.

The national government recognizes the duty of state governments to develop their services for diverse constituencies; to cooperate with the national government in achieving national goals; and to assist and coordinate the strengthening of local government.

Such a statement is needed as a beginning and a rallying point. It will hearten those who believe that the maintenance of a proper balance in the system, in cooperative attack on our problems, is essential to the preservation of our liberties and the expansion of our opportunities.

Third, Congress should establish a mechanism of govern-ment to function at the highest level of the executive branch, with sufficient presidential authority, to work daily to reduce conflicts, duplications, and confusion, and to exercise contin-uing initiative to reach the goals defined for intergovernmen-tal relations.

Senator Muskie said it this way:

It is time, then, that we fully recognize that this one man alone cannot coordinate the federal establishment and oversee the im-plementation of federal programs at the state and local levels. Constitutionally and politically, we have imposed an inordinate responsibility on the President to administer the laws that are to promote our national goals. He needs a mechanism for domestic affairs comparable to that available in foreign affairs.[15]

It is easy to become bogged down in the attempt to invent a new government mechanism to serve as coordinator and guardian of the federal system to set in order our intergov-ernmental relations. Senator Muskie has suggested a Na-tional Intergovernmental Affairs Council. Here are some of his words to describe both its organization and purpose, and his hope.

The council would be in the executive office of the Presi-dent, to "be chaired by the President and composed of those Cabinet officials and agency heads whose activities have a major impact on federal aid to states and localities and con-cern in intergovernmental relations." In addition there would be "an executive secretary directly responsible to the Presi-dent . . . [who] would speak for the President in develop-ing policy by which departments and agencies are to be coordinated and intergovernmental conflicts resolved." [16]

There is a danger that the executive secretary would be too far down the line to speak loudly enough. A powerless assistant was one cause of President Eisenhower's failure.

There is also danger that his staff would be hesitant to suggest drastic action, but would wait for the compromises and swap-offs urged upon the cabinet members by their departmental personnel. Effectiveness depends on the strength of the executive secretary and the commitment of the President.

A strong central arbiter ensconced in the White House could settle these interagency disputes over policy, procedures, and jurisdictions that now smolder unsettled for months . . . its clout would result from the President's personal involvement. "He's the only man who gives orders in this town, and even then it doesn't always work," one authority remarks.[17]

"The main point," Senator Muskie states, "is that the President would have a special assistant and an institution through which he could pull the federal establishment together and direct smoother intergovernmental implementation of federal aid programs." [18]

We also need an organization specifically studying intergovernmental relations, preferably authorized by Congress so that its work will be better received by the Congress and the White House. This means, in effect, that we need a continuation of the Advisory Commission on Intergovernmental Relations, with additional means provided to enable it to function more effectively. To absorb this function in some agency, or even in the White House, would be harmful, for the nonpartisan, relatively independent character of the ACIR has been one of its greatest assets in gaining wide acceptance of its contributions.

It is my observation that many officials in Washington are convinced of the urgency of improving state governments. Here is evidence from the testimony of John W. Gardner, Secretary of Health, Education, and Welfare, before Senator Muskie's subcommittee:

Most State and local governments are not strong enough to play their role in an effective partnership with the Federal Government.

They must be strengthened.

We must revitalize the State and local leadership so that it can play its role vis-à-vis an increasingly powerful Federal Government . . . without being completely submerged and obliterated. It is the only way to preserve our position of dispersed power and initiatives.[19]

This attitude spreading across the Washington scene will ultimately preserve the role of the states and will make "creative federalism" more than a mere phrase.

Another initial step, which could be guided by the National Intergovernmental Affairs Council, is to consolidate the numerous grant programs and arrange them in more understandable and less competitive patterns. There is a glimmer of hope on the horizon, already mentioned in the preceding chapter: the Comprehensive Health Planning and Public Health Services Amendments which provide for one grant to the state in place of nine previous grant-in-aid health-service programs. These "will be consolidated . . . [and] allocated in block for federally-approved state comprehensive plans developed to meet separate priority needs." [20]

It is possible that this may be the first tentative step down a new path for our federal grant system. Under this arrangement, the national government sets the broad national purposes and leaves development and administration of the specific program to the states. Since 1949, the President has had the power to reorganize executive departments of the federal government, subject to a congressional veto in sixty days. The President should be given the same authority for consolidating grants-in-aid—without altering the general purposes for which the funds were appropriated. This continuing ability to make programs more efficient is an appropriate executive function.

Here is a fourth central approach: *All bills before Congress involving intergovernmental relations should be considered in each house by the Government Operations Com-*

mittee in addition to the standing committe concerned with the substance of the legislation, for guidance as to consistency with the overall goals for enhancing a creative federalism.

To determine why the array of grant-in-aid programs and other intergovernmental programs are dissimilar and follow no pattern, it is necessary to understand the committee system of Congress. The authorizing committees, those dealing with a broad field of governmental interest, are concerned more with problems than with patterns. Usually the question before them is how to assist the state or the local government or some institution or some ongoing program, or to strengthen a weak endeavor. The committees naturally look for a solution to a particular problem. To find it is their primary concern, often difficult enough. There has been no requirement and perhaps little suggestion that they observe how the procedures match up with the other procedures instituted by other committees of Congress, agencies and departments, or even the same committee for some different problem.

I have been told by several congressmen that committee chairmen would never accept a suggestion that they align their procedures with those of other committees, or clear a bill with another committee for its intergovernmental impact. I don't know. They might welcome a chance to take part in better organizing the grant programs. I do not suggest that the Government Operations Committee should be able to bottle up legislation, or impede the flow of legislation to the floor, or even have the last word on intergovernmental structure and form. There is, however, an urgent need for greater uniformity, and it seems to me that it can be achieved only if there is one committee trying to achieve it. Such guidance would make no changes in the purposes of legislation or the level of appropriations. It would affect only the structure and procedures of the grant or program as it pertains to the relationship between the national government and the state or the local government or institution. It is unlikely that this guidance could be anything but helpful. Possibly the congressional leadership might find no need for a formal referral. Indeed it need not. It could be simply a staff service one committee provides for another. The members of Congress can work it out if they wish to do so.

In any event, whatever the practical difficulties in getting the principle of matched procedures accepted, it would be extremely beneficial to the states and cities, and the congressional intention itself would be more readily achieved if all congressional legislation affecting or employing intergovernmental relations followed the same general pattern and direction.

For all the improvement these four approaches might afford, our system can never reach the full potential of shared responsibilities unless the "outsiders" have a voice at the national level. It is argued that Congress effectively represents and reflects the thinking of the states. It does not do so and never has done so. Members of Congress do not represent state government and should not be expected to. They represent, for all their narrow district interests, the national view. They should.

This suggests a fifth central approach: *Chief executives of state and local government should be consulted prior to the President's request to Congress for the passage, extension, or change of grant programs affecting these governments.* This consultation need not be as clumsy as it might at first appear, assuming the President directed the consultation on the part of the national officials. I doubt if real consultation could be achieved in congressional hearings. They are concerned with presentation of positions in support of or opposition to a particular bill, more than with the details of drafting and preparation of ideas. The President could consult. Presidential briefing, as usually done, is not enough. It serves its purpose, but it is not what is required. The give-and-take of consultation is important.

The President has two former governors working as liaison

to the governors of the states.[21] They, working through the chairman of the Governors' Conference, could select several representative governors for consultation about any particular legislation. With advance information, the several governors could prepare for a conference. The President's liaison officers could meet them at some conference center, preferably away from the bustle of Washington, where the governors could discuss their views and advice. No one would expect the President to be bound by their views, but it is likely he would find them helpful. This process certainly would make use of a neglected resource in intergovernmental relations. The same group would not be called together for every problem. There could be changes in membership, and given all problems throughout a year, it is likely that most of the governors would be involved.

The guiding theme should be: "What can the states contribute, what administrative difficulties are presented, and how can the problems be attacked?" The consultation need not ask the question "Do you need money?" too often the only question now asked, with the answer known in advance.

The governors, mayors, and others outside of Washington have a tremendous amount of knowledge and experience which should be worked into planning legislation involving intergovernmental relations. The President's liaison officers could also consult by mail with all the other governors for help in addition to that received from the personal conferences. This process would make greater creative use of the liaison arm of the President's office. While it would put some burden on this office, it would be a relatively small burden in comparison with the benefits.

The President has already set the theme for appropriate consultation. In November, 1966, he sent a memorandum to the Secretaries of Commerce, Defense, HEW, HUD, Interior and Agriculture, the Attorney General, the Directors of OEO and the Office of Emergency Planning and the Bureau of the Budget, directing them to "take steps to afford rep-

representatives of the chief executives of state and local government the opportunity to advise and consult in the development and execution of programs which directly affect the conduct of state and local affairs." [22] This is excellent, but the process would be even more effective if the White House arranged the conferences.

We have talked about the laboratories of democracy the states once were, and to a degree are still. But the laboratories operate today in an atmosphere less free. This is not because there are deliberate restraints or because the states are no longer willing experimenters. It is because we have an intergovernmental relationship we did not have when La Follette was a governor.

The anti-poverty efforts furnish an illustration. Nothing much was being done about the "gray areas" of the cities until Paul Ylvisaker of the Ford Foundation and others began designing ways to help people break out of slums and environments of spiritual and economic poverty. Jobs, housing, remedial education, training for skills, out-of-the-way encouragement, and special attention to school children were the chief means. The several cities selected for pilot projects and supported by foundation funds were indeed laboratories. Here the remedies for poverty could be tried in limited areas.

North Carolina, in an attempt to turn these means to rural as well as city areas in a state-wide assault on the causes of poverty, looked at the experiments of the cities and sought the role of a state-sized laboratory in the democracy. To mount this attack the state of North Carolina in 1963 obtained a grant from the Ford Foundation and the Babcock and Reynolds foundations, with local matching funds and special grants from several federal agencies, to create a private and nonprofit organization known as The North Carolina Fund. It gave itself five years to try the new means of educating people out of poverty, hoping to find ways in which the regular health, education, employment, welfare, and related agencies on all levels of government might improve their reach.

This action was in the tradition of the state as a laboratory. It was all useful and instructive, and still is. But events will not always await experimentation. The explosive evils of slums and poverty required immediate attention, and within a year Congress appropriated, for an immediate national war on poverty, a thousand times the amount this laboratory was using. There was no time for more careful study and additional limited experiments. A crash experiment in every state was begun. Unfortunately there was an undeclared effort to eliminate state participation, but fortunately the program was begun with much flexibility, so that each state and each participating community could continue to carry on the experiment with considerable variations. OEO Director Sargent Shriver has developed remarkable impetus for the program, despite his lack of authority to coordinate related government activities. The program has been most successful, it is worth noting, in those communities where there is strong local support and in those states where the governor has fought his way into meaningful participation.

This indicates the intertwining pattern of governmental activities. No longer is it quite possible for a state to do much original experimentation in fields staked out by grant-in-aid programs. Yet some room remains for experimentation and innovation in methods and reach, and this room should be widened. It seems to me that some experiments must increasingly become intergovernmental undertakings, but that the states can still lead and originate, suggest and execute.

These thoughts lead me to one other recommendation worth trying. Several states might volunteer or be invited to serve as experimental laboratories for programs being or to be considered by the national Congress, so that the programs might be judged on the basis of experience and hard facts rather than debated on speculation. They could be refined and polished as needed, or discarded, before being put into practice across the nation. This is consistent with the methods of science.

There are a number of paths to intergovernmental experimentation. The food stamp plan, to assist low-income households to increase their expenditures for food and to upgrade the quality of their diets, was tried as a pilot project in eight areas across the nation. The plan is an alternative to the surplus food program, and permits the eligible households to exchange the amount of money they have been spending for food for an allotment of food coupons of higher monetary value. Purchases are made in regular retail stores at the prevailing retail price. Retailers redeem the coupons through the banks. This was a Department of Agriculture program, but arrangements were made for state departments of public welfare to administer the programs. The success of the pilot projects led to the passage of the Food Stamp Act of 1964, and in the spring of 1967 there were stamp programs operating in 680 areas in 41 states and the District of Columbia. This is an excellent example of interdepartmental and intergovernmental experimentation. This approach could be used for many ideas, and the originating partner could be either a state or a national agency.

In California an experiment was carried out with a demonstration project grant from the national government to develop a simplified procedure for determining eligibility for public assistance. After trying it for a year, California adopted the new process on a state-wide basis beginning April 1, 1967, and now some eighteen other states are experimenting with this new declaration form.

Experiments, under a grant from the Office of Juvenile Delinquency and Youth Development, prompted widespread changes in bail-bond procedures.

The national government has approached a number of problems with project grants, trying something new on a small scale first. Why not broaden this practice to larger issues and make it a permanent part of our intergovernmental techniques?

There are several areas of needed experimentation which could be initiated by a state or local government, or prompted by a federal agency. For example, these two could be considered: the negative income tax, or guaranteed minimum wage, and rent supplements. For focus I will quote William F. Buckley, Jr., on both these issues:

Granted, in our drive towards total welfarism we are entering a phase when we should seriously consider Prof. Milton Friedman's negative income tax proposal: drop all welfare programs and guarantee a minimum income to all family heads. . . .

Rent supplements to be used to permit the poor to live in privately owned dwellings are certainly an improvement on the notion of publicly owned housing.[23]

My purpose is not to debate the merits of either of these. There will be adequate debates in and out of Congress, and many doubts about taking such a national turnabout. A state willing to experiment would furnish facts for the debate.

The possibilities for increasing experimentation and stimulating fresh thinking in intergovernmental relations are almost limitless. The Congress could provide each cabinet member with some unrestricted funds he could use in the same way a private foundation uses its money—to finance experimental projects initiated by the state or local governments which do not come under any existing programs, or which suggest a promising variation. These funds would be available without much red tape on a matching basis, and their availability would surely unbridle state funds for additional experimentation. In short, the federal government would be matching ideas that came from state initiative, rather than the opposite. The plan might be structured so that the governors would go directly to cabinet officers without filtering their ideas through lower echelons. The states would know there was a source of funds to test new theories and approaches, and the federal government would have a constant means for the entry of fresh ideas from the states. The whole system would benefit.

Here, then, are five *central approaches* which could guide the efforts in Washington to improve intergovernmental relations in a fresh pattern. They will, if implemented, protect and defend our federal system against haphazard erosion. They are (1) presidential commitment, (2) a national policy, (3) a structure to implement presidential commitment, (4) a procedure to help Congress reach a consistent policy on national grants, and (5) a means for getting advice in advance from the states.

If the people of the United States want more effective state government, if they desire to preserve the federal system, these five broad approaches should guide the hundreds of steps required to reach those goals.

It is, when all is said, up to the people.

1. *Goals for Americans,* Report of the President's Commission on National Goals, (Englewood Cliffs, New Jersey: Prentice-Hall, Inc., 1960). p. 6.

2. For a discussion of these see: W. Brooke Graves, *Intergovernmental Relations, Their Origins, Historical Development, and Current Status,* (New York: Charles Scribner's Sons, 1964), Chapter 25, "The Search for an Acceptable Policy," pp. 884–910; and Morton Grodzins, *The American System, A New View of Government in the United States,* (Chicago: Rand McNally & Company, 1966), Chapter 12, "Centralization and Decentralization: The Failure to Unwind the System," pp. 307–326.

3. Speech, by Dwight D. Eisenhower, Republican Candidate for President, Des Moines, Iowa, September 18, 1952.

4. U.S. Commission on Intergovernmental Relations, *The Final Report of the Commission on Intergovernmental Relations,* (Washington: U.S. Government Printing Office, 1955).

5. *Ibid.,* p. 59.

6. *Ibid.*

7. *Ibid.,* p. 279.

8. *Ibid.,* p. vii.

9. "Atomic Energy Proposals," *State Government News,* Vol. X, (March 1967), p. 4.

10. U.S. Advisory Commission on Intergovernmental Relations, *State Agen-*

cies and Activities for Local Affairs: A Report (Washington: U.S. Government Printing Office, February 8, 1966), as reprinted in *The Congressional Record*, 89th Cong., 2nd Sess., Vol. 112, No. 36, March 1, 1966.

11. *Report of the Joint Federal-State Action Committee to the President of the United States and to the Chairman of the Governors' Conference*, (Washington: Progress Report No. 1, filed December, 1957, published, 1958).

12. See for example: *State Constitutional and Statutory Restrictions upon the Structural, Functional, and Personnel Powers of Local Government*, Report A-12, October, 1962; *State Constitutional and Statutory Restrictions on Local Taxing Powers*, Report A-14, October, 1962; *Apportionment of State Legislatures*, Report A-15, December, 1962; *The Problem of Special Districts in America*, Report A-22, May, 1964; *Metropolitan Social and Economic Disparities: Implications for Intergovernmental Relations in Central Cities and Suburbs*, Report A-25, January, 1965; *Federal-State Coordination of Personal Income Taxes*, Report A-27, October, 1965; *Intergovernmental Relations in the Poverty Program*, Report A-29, April, 1966; and an annual State Legislative Program with specific suggested legislation.

13. See for example: *Modernizing Local Government to Secure a Balanced Federalism*, (1966); *A Fiscal Program for a Better Balanced Federalism*, (1967), and *Modernizing State Government*, (1967).

14. *The New York Times*, January 15, 1967.

15. U.S. Congress, Senate, Subcommittee on Intergovernmental Relations of The Committee on Government Operations, *Hearings on Improving Intergovernmental Cooperation in the Management of Federal Assistance Programs, Creative Federalism Part I—The Federal Level*, 89th Cong., 2d. Sess., November, 1966, p. 7.

16. *Ibid.*, p. 5.

17. Jonathan Spivak, "Creative Federalism—A Big Administrative Mess," *The Wall Street Journal*, (New York), March 24, 1967, p. 6.

18. U.S., Congress, Senate, Subcommittee on Intergovernmental Relations, *op. cit.*, p. 5.

19. *Ibid.*, p. 268.

20. "Washington Report," *State Government News*, (November, 1966), pp. 9-10.

21. Farris Bryant of Florida and Endicott Peabody of Massachusetts.

22. "Steps Initiated to Implement 'Creative Federalism,' " *Congressional Quarterly*, Vol. XXV, No. 12, (March 24, 1967), p. 443.

23. William F. Buckley, Jr., Syndicated Column, *The Charlotte Observer*, (North Carolina), April 2, 1967.

CHAPTER XVI

The Tools of State Leadership

If the American people want their states to work in effective partnership for the good of the nation, there is no need to wait for word from Washington. The institutions that lead and guide the states can be revived, revamped, and developed to adult strength by state initiative.

The governorships, the legislatures, the constitutions, the personnel systems, the tax structures—indeed, every aspect of state government including the atmosphere of its activity —must be revitalized if states are to assume a new posture of leadership.

The branches of state government have been long at odds with one another on many questions involving the allocation of power. No branch of state government need be strengthened at the expense of any other. The tension that is necessary between the levels of government in a creative society must also be present within the states. Every part of state government must be energized. We need and must have vigorous state legislatures; but we need their vigor directed to legislative matters, not to tinkering with activities that properly belong to the executive.

After the Supreme Court jolted the temple with *Baker* v. *Carr*,[1] and called for reapportionment, the furious activity has been less than revolutionary in results, but there is every indication that the legislatures have begun to come to life and will get better.

Reapportionment focused attention on the legislatures as

never before. The intensive public airing of their weaknesses revealed problems so transparent and a legislative scene so permeated with archaic procedures and attitudes that all over the nation people interested in good government demanded reform.

The state legislatures are democracy's voice. The members frequently stand for election or re-election. They are seen and visited in their home communities at least on weekends during sessions, and daily in the months prior to the beginning of sessions. There cannot be many state legislators who have not been waited on by endless delegations either in support of or in opposition to some bill, seeking his assistance in getting a neighbor admitted to the state hospital, or soliciting his intervention with the governor on the matter of a bridge or a parole; who have not been telephoned by individuals, drunk or sober, at all hours of the night or early morning, written to by all manner of people, handed all assortments of brochures and briefs propounding some special project or program, and deluged with legislative bills and official documents. Most of them have little help in dealing with clerical matters, and even less help in studying the legislative matters. That they are frustrated is understandable. That they have, with all of their obstacles, and with the shortcomings in the help they have, and with the constant criticism, ground out most of America's progressive and useful legislation will be admitted by those who will look at the long record. In addition they have studied budgets and allocated money to the various priorities of state government in times of prosperity and in periods of economic depression.

Sometimes they have knuckled under to the special interests, sometimes they have voted with the winds of popular emotion, but the fact remains that they have put much honest and lasting legislation on the books. While they do have much influence on our daily lives, they seldom get praise for keeping our lives relatively simple; instead, they often get abuse for slowness and delay when the very purpose and mission of legislative bodies call for deliberateness and not speed. There is a good base on which to build better legislatures. They have not been the most effective group in government, but they have done better than many critics would have you believe. Neither have congresses, presidents, cabinet members, governors, university presidents, mayors, or other public officials maintained unblemished institutional records.

I contend that the legislatures of the states have the capacity to move into greater responsibility, and that they are in a position to play an important part in strengthening their executives, streamlining their governmental structures, reforming their constitutions, improving their personnel procedures, and providing the funds for adequate state services and aid to urban and other local governments. We have so much riding on state legislatures that they are going to have to rise to their challenges. I submit that they will, notwithstanding the enthusiastic invective that has been heaped upon them. The demands on them in the coming years are going to be tremendous if the states are to shore up the federal system. And the citizens, counting heavily on the state legislatures, as they must, would do well to give them all the support they will need. They have left themselves short of the tools they must have, and they do need citizens' backing now. John Anderson, a former governor of Kansas, now director of the Citizens Conference on State Legislatures, has pointed out:

The issues of salaries, staff, research, and offices, for example, are not minor matters. Research done by the Citizens Conference on State Legislatures indicates that the cost of operating the United States Congress is more than twice that of operating all 50 legislatures combined. Among other things, this is symbolic of the significance the country has come to attach to state government.[2]

I am not suggesting that the state legislatures match for themselves the appropriations Congress spends on itself. The states can do better with less, but they cannot do well enough with what they now have. California House Speaker Jesse Unruh has demonstrated how better pay, modern procedures, and adequate clerical, research, and office facilities can improve legislative effectiveness. So have other states. What is required is best reflected in the Final Report of the Twenty-Ninth American Assembly. From its eighteen cogent recommendations I have selected these as immediately important:

1. In many states, legislatures operate under severe constitutional limitations on their powers. . . . Constitutions should, however, leave legislatures as unhampered as possible, encouraging the development of their own self-reliance. Constitutional limits on the taxing power, constitutional earmarking of revenues . . . and other limitations on a legislature's power to appropriate public funds, and to address itself to public questions, should be eliminated.

2. The referendum should not be employed to reverse legislative decisions or to evade legislative responsibility. . . .

6. State constitutions should provide for periodic mandatory reapportionment. When initial responsibility for reapportionment is vested in a legislature, the authority and duty should be placed in a nonlegislative agency to effect the reapportionment should the legislature itself fail to do so.

8. Legislatures should be of a [smaller] size to make the position of legislators more important and visible. . . .

12. Competent professional staff should be provided the legislature. . . . In addition, legislatures should provide central services, including bill drafting, law revision, legislative library and reference services. Such central services should be staffed by professional personnel employed on a permanent nonpartisan basis. . . .

13. State legislators should be provided adequate offices. . . .

14. State legislators should utilize a strong system of standing committees, few in number, with broad, well-defined jurisdictions. . . .

16. . . . Efforts to define and control conflicts of interest have satisfied neither the public nor the legislatures. We recommend: First, codes of ethics. . . . Second, ethics committees . . . with advisory, review, and investigative functions which should extend to the activities of lobbyists. . . .

18. Legislative service will become more attractive when the public better understands the importance of legislatures in a democratic society. To improve this understanding, and to enhance the prestige of legislative service, programs should be undertaken to interpret the functions of state legislatures to and through mass media, and educational and civil institutions.[3]

These suggestions for reforms could not have been taken seriously ten years ago. It may be that the voters and legislators are now ready. The results, if they can be accomplished, will improve the quality of state legislation, the tone of state leadership, and the strength of the states' position. Far from restraining the governors, a renewed and refreshed legislature, armed with the means of modern government, will bring a vigorous effort to the same objectives the governors have. My guess is that legislative leaders will find governors willing workers for reforms of this kind.

It is equally true that the unhampered governor, far from restraining the legislatures, will open to them new channels of legislative strength and effectiveness.

The center of the state system, and its chief proponent in the eyes of the people, is the governor. The governor's prestige and his power to move people and ideas within his state are the strongest weapons in each state's arsenal. The future of the American system could well be determined by his performance.

The governor of every state has the potential for leadership. Whether he leads or not is determined by his own traits, the attitudes of his people, and the institutions of his state. But the potential is his. He is at once his party's political leader and his state's ceremonial head; he is the manager of state government and the molder of public opinion; he is the judge of demands and the responder to needs. It is the governor who must ask the people to do more. He must prod the institutions of state government to the service of the people.

The governor, by his very office, embodies his state. He stands alone at his inauguration as the spokeman for all the people. His presence at the peak of the system is unique, for he must represent the slum and the suburb, his concerns must span rural poverty and urban blight. The responsibility for initiative in major state-wide programs falls upon the governor. He must, like the President of the United States, energize his administration, search out the experts, formulate the programs, mobilize the support, and carry new ideas into action.

Few major undertakings ever get off the ground without his support and leadership. The governor sets the agenda for public debate; frames the issues; decides on the timing; and can blanket the state with good ideas by using his access to the mass media. He formulates the budget in most states; has the right to call special sessions of the legislature to focus attention and intensify pressure on a certain issue; can veto legislation in every state except one; and has an item veto on appropriations in forty-one of the fifty states. The governor is the most potent political power in his state. The harsh comments of just four or five can disturb the White House, and generate new concern and direct response, as was demonstrated by the special Governors' Conference of December, 1966.

Why, then, are governors so often unable to carry out the mission and the promise of the states? Are they held back by inadequate resources? Hemmed in by antiquated governmental structures and practices? The heirs of a historic but unrealistic distrust of an elected chief executive? Why do they find themselves in many places hamstrung by the poor image of state government, hindered by an indifferent public? Their failures are not always the fault of others. Often governors are either afraid or unwilling to lead their states as they should. The reason may be that they are a product of the system, too easily tossed by the winds of practical politics. The listing of "tax-loss" governors of the last few years is only one specter that strikes fear in the hearts of other governors. But a governor has no right to decline the hazards of leadership. Weak or ineffective gubernatorial leadership affects more than a state. It actually brings about a weaker federal sytsem and thereby a lesser nation than we might become.

Admittedly there is a tremendous variety among the states. In some states, the governor is strong and acts strong. In others he is weak. Sometimes the weakness is one of personality. The voters' attitudes affect that. But regardless of personality, he must be given the means to lead. He represents not only the best hope of the state, but the pivot of a federal system with the tensions, competitions, and conflicts from which flow innovative solutions to American problems.

In the fall of 1965 I asked the governors: "What powers, both formal and informal, do you lack which could aid you significantly in effecting your programs?"

They see their own problems as organizational, usually with such impediments as prohibition on running for re-election; too many boards and commissions; too many other elected officials; figurehead lieutenant governors; lack of continuity and coordination of departments; and inadequate appointment and removal powers. Or they see them as financial: too much earmarking of funds, no item veto, constitutional restrictions on taxes and borrowing, insufficient revenues under their control, and lack of adequate control of the budget. Or as problems of legislative relations: apportionment, too short sessions, biennial sessions, legislative interference. The answers break down roughly into a half-dozen categories: organizational problems within the executive branch; financial problems; legislative relations problems; political problems; intergovernmental problems; and problems in state programs. In summary, it is clear: the states are not alike, but all need to help themselves in differing ways.

The secret to self-help is leadership, and the governor is responsible for leadership within each state. To be able to lead, the governor needs to be freed from the barbed wire of antiquated constitutional barriers. He needs to have brought back to him the slices of executive authority which have been handed other elected officials or boards and commissions. He needs restored to him the reins of scattered budget authority, and to be relieved of practices in the selection of personnel which prevent efficient operation of his administration.

He must have the tools he needs to lead effectively: an executive budget; a modern civil service; a strong planning process close to the governor; fewer elective offices; a lieutenant governor who can share some of the executive burden; fewer boards and commissions controlling the administration of departments; and sufficient staff to maintain an effective governor's office. There are other needs, but these represent necessities for management if a state chief executive is to be effective.

The particulars of a state reform program will have to be hammered out in each state. Many have on file the recommendations of "Little Hoover Commissions," blue-ribbon committees, as well as books and articles by members of the academic community. For some, the problems are apparent; others must initiate studies.

I have brought together ten recommendations. If these are achieved, along with improvements in legislatures and revision of the state tax structure, the states will have preserved the federal system by strengthening themselves—regardless of the reluctance of the national government.

It is my own conclusion that there is one single key that will open the first door leading to adequate and effective state government. It is simple.

1. *Make the chief executive of the state the chief executive in fact.* The executive should be given executive authority, and then held responsible by the voters for the efficiency, the accomplishments, and the honesty of his operation of government.

The executive authority and effectiveness of the national government have grown simultaneously over the past century, and this growth has been especially rapid in the last thirty years. A noted political scientist remarked to me that, because of the machinery for the operation of government which surrounds him, it is almost impossible now for a President to be a weak or bad President—although, he added, some have tried mighty hard.

From the beginning, the executive authority of the state governors has been circumscribed. "The early state constitutions . . . relegated the governorship to a position of complete insignificance. . . . The mainspring—the dominating force in the political machinery—of early American government was the legislature." [4] Gradually some governors have unshackled the office from these early constraints—but in some states, relics of the past remain. Few governors are supported by such institutionalized machinery as the President has, and it is quite possible to have a weak or bad governor.

We often see a strong governor in a state followed by a weak or ineffective one. The strength of a governor must too often rest in personality or public appeal, or force of conviction, or emergencies which coalesce support for needed action. His achievement too often is personal and not, as in the Presidency, that of his executive office and its supporting institutions.

We can preach and pray for strong governors with the capacity to furnish the leadership needed by the states. Occasionally we get them. But if we want the office, as distinguished from the individual, to carry the strength of confidence, then we need to provide the same kind, if not the degree, of institutional support that upholds the presidency.

Talk about structures and reorganization has only academic meaning unless we realize that the purpose of the recommended changes is to give to the office the strength which will enable an ordinary man to provide good leadership and an extraordinary man to provide brilliant leadership.

2. *State constitutions, for so long the drag anchors of state progress, and permanent cloaks for the protection of special interests and points of view, should be revised or rewritten into more concise statements of principle.*

There is not much possibility of generalization on what should be done to a particular constitution. State constitutions exhibit too many dissimilarities. Many states are now trying to capture the imagination of the people to bring their basic legal document up to date.

The need for revision does not rest upon the mere fact that the document is long, involved, or frequently vague. Rather it rests upon what the constitution contains that thwarts the functioning of state government, the blocks thrown in the way of efficient operation.

An old constitution need not be scrapped because it is antiquated, but it may be revised to meet new needs. Some state constitutions were originally written to deal in detail with particular situations in a way that the passage of time has made increasingly awkward or unworkable. One governor wrote me:

. . . I am sure that I will not be the only Governor to give highest priority to the need for a study of constitutional inhibitions that serve as obstacles to the solution of new state problems. Constitutional tax limits, constitutionally earmarked funds, and the like, were obviously written into the basic state document at other times to serve other needs. They often serve in the present to impede state action in vital, new areas of governmental concern.[5]

3. *The two-year term for governors should be replaced with a four-year term, and a governor should be allowed to seek to succeed himself at least once. Maybe, if succession is not favored in some states, a six-year single term might be considered.*

Whatever else stays, the two-year term should go. People who favor it do not want states to act effectively or do not believe in the federal system. By the time a two-year governor takes office, he must start running again. By the time he gets a program suggested, he is out of office, or his re-election is an open question, or his motives are being questioned in a campaign by his political opponent. He must be a constant re-electioneerer. That governors survive the ordeal of the governorship in states with two-year terms is a credit to their strength of personality and leadership, or a tribute to their ability to fade imperceptibly out of public debate without laying a hand on any project. Years ago, when men had more reason to fear tyranny, a two-year term seemed, perhaps, a safeguard of liberty. We even had some one-year governorships. Now all but ten states elect governors for four-year terms.[6]

Of the forty states that have a four-year term, only twelve now provide that the governor may not succeed himself.[7] In two of the two-year states there is also a four-year limit.[8] Some good reasons for this restriction may have existed in the early days of the nation. The limitation was based on the common feeling that the governors should be restricted because the colonial governors had been entrenched and oppressive. The legislative devices cut the governor down to subservient size. Unfortunately, they were unable to foresee that it would also cut the legislatures down to a smaller size. A strong executive helps develop a strong legislative branch. Neither can rise or fall alone.

Getting programs going and moving an inert bureau toward getting its work done are more likely if the governor can stay around long enough. The approval or disapproval for continuing a program can be decided by the voters at the mid-point, but the program has a better chance if it is possible for the governor to succeed himself. If the governor can be trusted, he can be trusted to stand for re-election at least once. Succession is not a right given to a governor; it is a right retained by the people—the right to choose whomever they want as their governor. While other factors enter, in those states where at least eight years of service is possible without the disruption of an election every two years, the results of government generally have been better.

This limitation has been particularly devastating in the South where all but three states have a one-term limitation. This limiting clause is now almost exclusively a Southern feature. There is no apparent reason for the South to punish itself by placing such a limitation on leadership. As David Broder has observed about one of these states, it "is one of those benighted states that supposes it saves itself from tyranny by denying its most competent officials a chance to serve a second consecutive term."[9]

In the past two years Massachusetts, Michigan, Nebraska, and North Dakota have moved to four-year terms, with no limitation on the number of terms. Louisiana, Pennsylvania, and Missouri have removed the one-term limit in favor of a two-term limit. The trend is in the direction that will benefit the states—away from two-year terms and one-term limitations.

4. *The governor should be given the dominant authority in the budget process, preferably as budget director.*

There is no way the governor can effectively plan and

coordinate unless he makes up and controls the budget. Money is the principal source of strength in action of any kind. The budget direction allows him to avoid duplication. More important, it makes all agency and department heads unusually responsive. No executive can be very effective unless he has control of the budget. In addition to the authority, he needs an adequate budget staff and assistants. I have seen the governor of a major state with budget papers spread out over his desk, scribbling details with a lead pencil. The budget is the foundation of all state services, and it must be treated with major seriousness.

5. *The governor, as chief planner for his state, must conduct his administration to enable his state to look beyond his term of office to the future.* Few governors concern themselves with planning, for planning simply to help the next governor seems irrelevant to the everyday tasks that pile up in a busy governor's office. We are really talking about the future result of present policy decisions—the long-term effect of today's decisions.

Presently, state planning is often limited to the accumulation of various budgetary decisions to withhold or give money to carry out this or that proposal. The decisions follow no real guidelines toward recognized long-range state goals. Without the guides, decisions are based on the prior year's budget plus a nominal expansion of the agencies' activities. It is no surprise that a recent study of the states' expenditures for the 1929–1962 period concluded that "Decisions made in the past appear to be the hardiest and most frequently used touchstone for current budgeting." [10] These decisions are usually made by agency budget officers rather than the members responsible for policy and development. In essence, budget officers often make policy rather than serve as a staff for the policy makers. States must develop a planning mechanism which uses all the means available, not just the budget process.

Governors need new ways to test the complex results of

their decisions. A governor must develop an understanding of the interrelationships of all our governmental activities, and must be able to predict the effect of each on the long-range goals of the others. We know that roads and electric power attract industry, but we must come to understand that a good state school system materially helps industrial growth also. We must develop ways of measuring the extent to which the availability of recreational, cultural, and amusement facilities affect mental-health programs; and again, the cost of a stream or a beach ruined for recreation by industrial waste. Somehow, we must develop a new kind of accounting system —a system that measures what it will cost us to solve a problem against what it will cost us to do nothing.

Planning is a never-ending, dynamic process for bringing about the changes necessary to reach desired goals. The product of a state's efforts must be a coordinated and *comprehensive planning process*, not a plan. If a plan is a necessity in some cases, it must be conceived as a by-product of the process, subject to such continual updating and necessary change that it can never become the rationale for maintaining the *status quo*. Planning could be likened to keeping a loose-leaf notebook for each major state responsibility, with new leaves inserted almost daily, so that at any time the policy makers have available the facts, choices, and alternatives for decision.

To be effective, planning must be at the governor's right hand. He is the only person with the power to bring agencies together, determine priorities, and smooth out conflicts. And he needs to be able to get his information quickly and accurately.

We talked with one innovative aide to a governor who tried to give us his view of the near future:

I would like to see a briefing room, similar to the war room at the Pentagon. Slides, maps, graphs, and information would be constantly stored by computer and updated for the governor's use. If he asked what the story was on school dropouts, we could give him the latest rates, what kind of kids, how we compare with other states, federal programs available, the status of our grant requests, state programs in this field, etc., all pictorially presented for ready use. We could provide him and his staff with the history of our state's activity in the field in question, and list reports they ought to prepare. And perhaps present some recommendations or alternative suggestions which had come from past commissions, private groups, and individuals which had never been implemented. The governor could then decide which way he wanted to go. But he would always have the latest information in the field.[11]

This may seem somewhat theatrical for some states, but there are many other ideas for giving the governor the facts to fight with. The beginning point is the appreciation by the states themselves of the governor's role as chief planner for the state, and of planning as an essential part of leadership.

6. *Like the President of the United States, each governor should have the authority to reorganize and regroup his executive agencies, subject to legislative veto within a specified period of time.*

All governments tend to set up agencies and divisions within departments in order to spotlight problems and aim appropriations right at a problem that may have momentarily captured public attention. Legislators constantly introduce bills to set up new departments, upgrade current departments, break them up, rename them, reshape their emphasis, and redefine their goals. The result is recurring overlap and duplication; a loss of focus as programs are dribbled out through too many agencies. The inevitable scenario is familiar: advisory committees, committees for cooperation, and joint committees for communication between agencies.

Reorganization is in the first instance a management problem, typically the function of executives whether in business or government. A governor should not be forced to toss reorganization into the legislative mill with the rest of his requests because there will always be higher priorities in his legislative program. It is too easy to say "Let's limp along a little longer" for something as colorless as reorganization of government.

For effective coordination instead of proliferation of state agencies and departments, constant and clean-cut regroupings are needed. Experience has shown it to be difficult, if not impossible, to accomplish needed regroupings by sporadic legislative act. Government becomes unmanageable as it grows. The governor's authority is the counterforce to bring order into the process.

The length of time for legislative review would have to be set by the state legislatures in some relation to the sessions of the legislature, but this time period could be established according to the schedules in each state.

The national government, acting upon the recommendations of the Hoover Commission, granted this authority to the President. By executive act the structure can be kept in working order. Since the Executive Reorganization Plan of 1949, through the administrations of four presidents, there have been more than sixty proposals for reorganization. For a governor to have to make reorganization a part of his legislative program, when he is already overburdened with substantive programs and legislative messages, simply means that reorganization will be delayed until next term or passed on to the next governor, who, faced with the same problems, seldom gets time for reorganization. Seven states have given their chief executives the power to reorganize.[12] The other states should follow their lead.

7. *The executive committees, state councils, and separately elected executive officers and independent boards and commissions should be eliminated, in authority if not in fact.*

If there is divided authority there can be no final responsibility. The people are entitled to know where the responsibility for governmental activities resides, but they cannot know unless they insist on constitutional and legislative reform placing the executive duties in the hands of the chief executive. Furthermore, the hobbles of split authority make it difficult for a governor to lead. One of the basic causes of inefficiency in state government, of the inability to venture away from the dead center, and of leaving the initiative to the national government, is that there are too many engineers in the state cab with their own throttles and brakes.

It doesn't matter that a department head is selected by a board, if the board is in turn responsive to the governor. But the very existence of an independent board or commission usually means that the departmental executive and his department are screened from any gubernatorial direction.

Senator Mark Hatfield, as he was leaving the governor's office in Oregon after eight years, wrote:

Our greatest disappointments, however, came in the basic structure of state government itself. Oregon has an archaic organization which makes administration exceedingly difficult. We have in excess of 100 different boards, agencies, and commissions that report to the governor. Many of these are virtually independent of any control by the chief executive. This has resulted in an inefficient, uneconomic, and unresponsive structure and any success in administration is in spite of the problems built into the organization. . . . In my opinion sound organization would naturally strengthen state government and place it in a position to play more adequately its proper role.[13]

In nine states commissioners of insurance are elected. There is no pattern for cabinet level selection, as in the national government. Five commissioners of labor are elected. But this does not mean that the governors appoint all the others. Eight officials charged with regulations of public utilities are elected. The head of one highway department is elected. No welfare director is elected, but two are appointed by the governor subject to council approval, two are subject to departmental board approval, one is subject to approval by either house, fifteen are subject to senate approval, and eight are without any further approval; in addition a commission appoints two, and sixteen are appointed by boards, two of whom must be approved by the governor and one of whom must be approved by the senate. There is no uniform pattern, even within a single state. Governors appoint twenty-one commissioners of agriculture. No approval is required in five states, but in eleven these commissioners must be approved by the senate, in one by either house, in two by a board, and in two by a council. Twelve are elected by the people, eight by constitutional requirement, and four by statute.[14]

These samplings are random, but generally typical. I do not suggest uniformity among the states in the selection of officers. It probably makes little difference how the secretary of state is elected or selected. The selection of the secretary of state is a matter of concern, however, in those states where he is granted some executive authority. The problem lies not in his selection, but in giving an officer executive duties that properly belong to the chief executive.

No citizen of any state should tolerate the diffusion of command, the division of authority, or the hamstringing of executive power. The head of a corporation could not run his firm if the vice president in charge of sales were elected by the board, the superintendent of production selected by the vice presidents with the approval of the president, the transportation chief by the union members, and the personnel director by a visiting committee.

If the citizens want the governor to govern, they cannot afford to distribute his duties among other elected officials, and among boards and commissions chosen in an assortment of ways, accountable to nobody knows whom.

8. *Merit systems and civil service, a strength for government when properly structured, must be disentangled from an overzealous past, and liberated from an overprotective philosophy that smothers the best talent, prevents rapid promotions, and often penalizes assertive leadership.*

The nature of the personnel problem has changed because government has changed. The problem for an incoming administration is no longer finding top-level jobs for friends, but convincing people to serve. It is no longer "cleaning house" of enemies, but finding capable people to do increasingly complex and challenging jobs. Party label is less relevant. Ability is the new premium. As a Midwest director of administration described his merit system: "Most civil-service systems are still geared to 'keeping rascals out' and 'holding them down.' We've got to figure out a way to bring talent in and move them up." Good people do not want to join a lock-step personnel system in which promotions are as sure as the seasons and longevity the only test of recognition.

Top-level administrators in almost every state complained about the restrictiveness of the existing personnel systems. Governors felt that energizing their own departments was one of their most difficult tasks, and many strongly felt the frustration of trying to innovate in a system over which they had only the most minimal authority. A governor of one of our small states told me, "I can appoint my press secretary and that's about it." This may be an extreme case, but the point is significant. The assistant commissioner of education in a state with a national championship football team understands the problem: "The governor should have the appointive power of his key administrative people in all departments. Football coaches bring in all their assistants. We wouldn't think of tying them to a merit system or civil service for the second level. They come in as a team and we hold the head coach responsible. But then, football's important, isn't it?" In our zeal to keep politics out and protect the governmental employee, we have in many places allowed the merit system to become a virtually impregnable thicket.

A recent survey on behalf of a national agency demonstrated that state departments of health are "woefully inadequate." One reason is that departments of health over the years have been over-professionalized. The process began with the pretense that health is too important to be left to the politicians. This, of course, is true. But a qualification of that sentence was left off and overlooked in most states. Public health is too important to be left to the professionals—or for that matter to any one group except the public.

This trend has been evident in many other fields of endeavor. Welfare and education suffer the restraint of over-professionalization in most states. Not only the staff but the governing board itself has often shielded itself from the hand and eye of the public. Were these boards truly independent, the effect would not be deadening. Too often they become "dependent" boards, harking to the direction of the professionals. Their department's constituency has ceased to be the people they serve, but has become the professional interests. The boards have cut themselves off from the public, and the process is circular. They belong to their constituencies and their constituencies belong to them. Where is the public in this merry-go-round?

No wonder state government has failed to develop more vigorous departments. There are notable exceptions, and many sensitive, responsive, and creative professionals work in state government, seriously and without adequate recognition. The protection of the professional is essential and beneficial if the activity is the kind that should, traditionally, be shielded from direct political action—law enforcement, the schools, and the colleges are good examples. Traditionally, we do not expect political interference with the state university board, and should not tolerate board interference with administrative and academic procedures. There must, however, be an involvement by political leadership in university and education improvement. I favor block appropriations to state universities, but I do not suggest complete divorcement from political interest. More universities have suffered from political indifference than have ever been upset by political interference. There has been political abuse of professionals, but the public is more aware and less indulgent of raw interference. The public is well served by professionals who work in a climate of freedom from political hackism, but it is also served if there is a means of disturbing the professional who is unconcerned for the broader picture and the higher aims.

It is not desirable or even possible to adopt a uniform pattern of personnel management across the country. Particulars are not so important as principles, and we can tolerate many variations. We need a living personnel system to provide more adequate salary levels, rational routes of promotion, imaginative recruitment processes, a "court" to press grievances, and new training programs. We need a twofold system enabling a governor to appoint and remove those officials who have the power to formulate and administer his policies, but maintaining the security of the career employee. Better government is not served when personnel policy and law permit the civil servant to be badgered and harassed by politicians. On the other side, the career employee must not be entirely isolated from political influences; for government must be responsive and always open to the possibility of change. This is a delicate balance and a fine line to draw.

9. *The governor must have adequate staff to represent adequately the public interest.*

Governors and the legislators have been unusually sensitive about the governor's staff. Both have been afraid of the criticism following additions of new staff positions. It caused less of a stir if the governor got along with the number his predecessor used.

Demands on all state governments, regardless of the size of the state, are increasing; and the states that try to operate with the traditional small staff find themselves overloaded.[15]

The people and the newspapers and the legislatures should understand that the executive functions cannot be performed without adequate help. The myth that the governor alone can solve thousands of problems personally is part of the old timidity that holds us back. A recent study of fourteen governors' offices concluded:

As a state grows, the demands placed on the governor necessitate more help in running the office. In the states studied, the smallest office is composed of three professionals, while more than a hundred people, professional and secretarial-clerical, managed the largest. If we ignore the very large states, the average number of staff members (counting only the professionals) is usually six or seven.[16]

We have moved beyond the day when a governor's office staff could consist of a legal assistant and an administrative assistant, plus a few secretaries.

The governor's need for a staff begins on election day. Too many governors-elect have to use whatever leftover campaign money they can find to run their offices between election and inauguration. Congratulations inundate the newly elected governor; the budget needs his decisions; he must decide on program directions; and he must assemble his administration. Every state should provide him the necessary funds, offices, secretarial help, and staff for this "in-between" time before he takes office. In addition, immediately after the election, he should be given access to primary information and plans relating to the budget, the personnel system, and individual departments and agencies. In short, we must realize that the governor-elect must get ready to be governor in many ways before his inauguration.

The handicaps in this role during the transition between administrations must be removed.

10. *The governor's office should be organized to be receptive to new ideas and should use the experiences of other states in seeking fresh solutions to problems.*

An aide to a Midwestern governor said to me, "I think every governor needs someone on his staff whose only job is to gaze out the window and brood about the future." The best executives, in or out of government, are those receptive to fresh ideas, unafraid to seek out something different. There are not, unfortunately, anything like enough good executives, in or out of government. An idea has no added value just because it is new; it might well be that the old way is far better. The creative executive, however, carries on a constant testing of ideas, a questioning of old approaches, an inquiring with open mind. The public has no sure way of judging such creative executive qualities in advance. Some of the brightest-looking candidates have turned out to be the most timid and cautious executives. Something about the responsibilities of office paralyzed them. They wouldn't change the hands on a slow clock, let alone rewrite the procedures for a grant-in-aid program. We need executives in the statehouses, in the cabinet chairs, in the city halls, who have inquiring, open, bold minds, undaunted by new ideas. There are numerous ways a governor can invite, seek out, and receive the workings of bright minds. I make no plea for specific devices. I simply suggest several.

Some governors have used scholars, faculty members, industry researchers, writers, and other citizens to meet periodically with him for freewheeling discussions of a particular subject or a broader field, or the whole range of government. What the governor has done is to bring to himself people concerned with government, students of considerable note in many cases, who have no real outlet for their ideas, especially not in a place where they ever see any effect. They themselves may have been laboring under mistaken notions, but in the bumping of idea against idea, the clash of thoughts and arguments, lie the beginnings of improved action. A governor is necessarily busy, day and night, hour after hour, and no matter how hard he works he will never do all he wants to do or meet all the demands placed upon him. But if he somehow finds time for the lively exchange of ideas with men of theory, he will serve his state better than if he plods through the routine tasks of his office with his eyes down on the furrows.

There is also a mass of material, with direct relevance to the day-to-day job of the governor, which a busy governor finds it difficult to examine. As former South Carolina Governor Ernest F. Hollings said to me, "A governor has stacks of written material full of all kinds of valuable information. But it is like trying to take a drink of water out of a fire hydrant. And about the time you begin to understand some of these things—you are out of office."

The Council of State Governments, the governors' own organization, publishes with regularity materials and magazines with advice and suggestions of daily value. Yet I have had a number of governors tell me that they seldom find it possible to read all this material.

This neglect reflects no lack of interest or lack of concern, but a lack of time. A governor may lack the time to read and ponder because he lacks an adequate staff. I am satisfied that every governor could use an aide in his office to look at publications relevant to the governor's job. He could summarize, mark, discard, and call useful ideas to the governor's attention with written comments. He would bring many excellent ideas before the governor while they might yet be useful to him. Better yet, he could verbally brief the governor in bits of otherwise wasted time, for instance, when the governor may be en route to make a speech at a convention of basket weavers. There is no reason why this duty should be placed in a formal structure; probably his relation with the governor should be totally informal. The need is that a "surveyor of knowledge" be included in the governor's staff.

A governor needs all possible ways to gather additional ideas. One source would be people invited not to make speeches, but to sit with the governor and a small group of administration leaders and talk over some part of government and its future. The next few years will bring dramatic changes in state government, and governors will need new, sound ideas to guide these changes.

We need to institutionalize the open door to ideas, however hinged, beyond the formal planning departments, beyond casual perusal. Through seeking out new ideas, experiences, and approaches, the governor will be able to help the state serve its innovative purpose in the federal system.

These are not all of the improvements needed in the executive branch of state government. Some of them are not needed in some states, which already operate in the suggested manner, or perhaps in a way that is much better. Some states are doing all these things and more. I have selected essentials, the minimum, the starting point toward putting the executive in a position best to serve the people of his state. Always the basic need remains leadership. Governors, given the means for management and leadership, can and must lead their states along the road toward vital, essential participation in the task of redeeming and saving the American system and the American tradition.

Governor Nelson Rockefeller of New York has said: "One of the principal suggestions I would make to all states and all governors is the exercise of leadership to attack the problems of the public even though this means facing up to fiscal realities." [17] In other words, the governors must make hard fiscal and other decisions and often take temporarily unpopular stands in order to lead effectively. Leadership by the governor is the first essential for the revitalization of the federal system. Leadership does not result merely from the courage of the governor. It requires a sounder state structure. Governor Calvin Rampton of Utah summed it up:

It is my belief that the organizational structure of our State Government is at fault. Through a fear of strong government, we have placed so many safety valves in the governmental system that we can never get any steam in the boiler—never take the steps necessary to satisfy the public desire for action or to keep our State Government abreast and ahead of the game. Consequently the people lose even more faith in their State Government, and turn more frequently to the federal system for aid in solving what are basically state problems.[18]

But structure and organization alone are not enough. The states, more than anything else, need leaders strong and unafraid, willing to try new ideas and seek new paths, determined to make their states worthy of the name, to arouse the people to their opportunities, and to fulfill the role of the states in the American federal system.

1. *Baker* v. *Carr*, 369 U.S. 186 (1962).
2. John Anderson, "On Behalf of the States," *National Civic Review*, Vol. LV, (January, 1966), p. 11.
3. *State Legislatures in American Politics*, Report of the Twenty-ninth American Assembly, (New York: The American Assembly, Columbia University, 1966), pp. 5–9, *passim*.
4. Duane Lockard, *The Politics of State and Local Government*, (New York: The Macmillan Company, 1963), pp. 345–346.
5. Letter from Robert E. Smylie, Governor of Idaho, October 27, 1965.
6. Those states without four-year terms are: Arizona, Arkansas, Iowa, Kansas, New Hampshire, New Mexico, Rhode Island, South Dakota, Texas, and Vermont. *Book of the States, 1966–1967*, (Chicago: The Council of State Governments, 1966), p. 137.
7. Those states in which the governor may not succeed himself are: Alabama, Florida, Georgia, Indiana, Kentucky, Mississippi, North Carolina, Oklahoma, South Carolina, Tennessee, Virginia and West Virginia. *Ibid.*

206 / *Storm Over the States*

8. The two states are New Mexico and South Dakota. *Ibid.*
9. David Broder, "Political Parade," the *Washington Post*, April 4, 1967.
10. Ira Sharkansky, "Correlates of State Government Expenditures," paper delivered at the 1966 Annual Meeting of the American Political Science Association, New York, September, 1966.
11. Interview with Phillip V. Maher, Director of the Office of State and Regional Planning and former special assistant to Governor Warren Hearnes of Missouri, January 11, 1967.
12. Those states which give the governor the power to reorganize subject to legislature review are: Alaska, Kentucky, Massachusetts, Michigan, New Hampshire, Oregon, and Pennsylvania. *Modernizing State Government*, (Washington: The Committee for Economic Development, 1967), p. 53.
13. Letter from Mark O. Hatfield, U.S. Senator, State of Oregon, February 3, 1967.
14. *Book of the States, 1966–1967*, p. 139.
15. Alan J. Wyner, "Governor–Salesman," *National Civic Review*, Vol. LVI, (February, 1967), p. 82.
16. *Ibid.*
17. Letter from Nelson A. Rockefeller, Governor of New York, November 16, 1965.
18. Letter from Calvin L. Rampton, Governor of Utah, October 25, 1965.

CHAPTER XVII

United Purpose

From the beginning of the nation there has been a running conflict between the federalist point of view and the republican (as Jefferson called it) point of view. The anti-federalist attitude was something different from either, and has long since disappeared. It has not been my intention to carry forward the "compact versus union" debate, but rather to attempt discovery of the uniting features which have been evolving for a century or more. I have no doubt that we do indeed have a national government, with national impulses, seeking national goals, and generally and broadly supported by the citizens who believe that the opportunities and liberties of all people in all parts of the nation should be promoted and protected. The idea of the national government with national drive comes from Hamilton's federalist concepts. It may come from Edmund Burke and John Adams, but Hamilton is its symbol. For the most part Abraham Lincoln, Theodore Roosevelt, and Franklin Roosevelt are the latter-day apostles, and it was the party of Thomas Jefferson that first found the way to make the Hamiltonian concept, the national idea, a working policy. No one is likely to deny that both political parties now espouse the national idea, and it is our accepted public policy.

However, our acceptance of the national idea in its modern development brought about by our responses to the expanding complexities of industrial world leadership, does not imply that we have abandoned the republican ideas of

Jefferson. I think we have not, and as I observe what is happening in our country, I see no inclination to drop them. In fact, I gather we cherish them even more, realizing that they define our new national idea in a way that supports our basic desire for freedom, individualism, privacy, and liberty.

We have dropped the elite aspects of Hamilton's thinking, and we have dropped the "old fatal policy of drift" that was inherent in Jefferson's approach. We retain the concept of one nation with a national government dedicated to promoting the national aspects, and we retain the Jeffersonian concern for all people, and his trust in democracy.

My home town was called Cross Creek in colonial days, and it is situated in what is still called Cross Creek Township, both named after a stream that crossed another in a most peculiar way. The Scotch Highlanders found them at the head of boat navigation on the Cape Fear River where they settled. The two streams ran together but did not join. Rather they crossed each other with such individuality that a stick thrown in Cross Creek flowed across Blount's Creek, and the waters of Blount's moved undeflected through Cross Creek. Downstream the two creeks united to flow together to the Cape Fear River and toward the ocean.

The doctrines of Jefferson and Hamilton flowed from different directions, crossed but retained their separateness, and have ultimately come together to flow within the same banks.

Superficially, it is possible to miss the unity. That the liberal has not been true to Jefferson, the conservative has departed from Hamilton, is frequently asserted. Also the loose contention is sometimes made that Hamilton is the true ancestor of the New Deal, while it is equally contended that Jefferson's concern for the common man made him the prophet of the New Deal. The truth is that both were, and that neither Hamilton nor Jefferson knew the words *liberal* and *conservative*, that neither did more than struggle with the best vision available at the time to shape the purposes as they believed they should be. Today Hamilton's confidence in the nation and Jefferson's confidence in the people are finally joining.

Neither man, we might speculate, would be unduly disturbed today upon hearing the complaint that the two great political parties are not very far apart in what they stand for. While speculation would not be so brash as to put them in the same political party today, it is true that their principles are in both parties.

With the coming of the technological revolution, it is good to know how close we have come together. We must exercise what deftness is possible in political action and interaction to make certain that the best features of both philosophies are used to preserve our federal system.

The shadowy outlines of the future are sharpened day by day, and with emerging clarity we begin to see the forms of dome-covered cities, agriculture without soil, commercial rocket travel, drugs which alter personality, control of the weather, and containment of the population explosion. With all these perplexing influences on man's life, it is predictable that our system of government will adjust and readjust. Where weaknesses and inequities show, they will be corrected or overcome. The forms of our government will remain, in deference to history, but their role in the technological tomorrow will be set by our concern of today.

We have moved to the national idea in an irreversible way, so the demand of future generations on us is that we harness, while we are able, the powers of our system in a manner that combines our values of individual liberty with maximum opportunity. The American people understand that the way we disperse power determines the place of the individual in his government. That was the reason for the establishment of three branches within the national government, and the basis of the compromise which left the states with considerable political power. If power flows to power, and it does, then our task is not to engage in a futile fight to weaken the national idea, but rather to seek intelligent ways to keep our power plural. This will require a conscious and even determined combination of efforts to restrain the accumulation of more and more magnetizing power in one place of government.

Our whole history, and our political philosophy, is a monument to the belief that power is limited, and that power should be limited. . . . The American position was, quite simply, that no government had all power. That is part of the meaning of our written constitutions—documents which enumerate with greatest care the powers which governments may exercise. That is the heart of our elaborate system of checks and balances—the determination to limit the authority and the power of government. That is what the bill of rights, state and federal are about—limitations on government. . . .[1]

The federal system, preserved as a federal system, is the institution of restraint. The competitive governments serve not only to restrain absolute power, they serve positive purposes as well. The internal clashes and conflicts promote the creative tension that adds to the competitive features in a constructive manner. With weak state governments, the tension is less, and there is less challenge and weaker competition. It is as if a runner sought to set a world record without anyone pressing him to do his best. Without the tension of competition, the whole race is slower.

Liberals and conservatives do not disagree on all matters, and especially need they not disagree on the historic form of our federal government. Most perceptive liberals and conservatives today see the wisdom of strengthening state government as part of a more effective federal system of government. To paraphrase into today's terminology Jefferson's commentary on the federalists and the republicans in his first inaugural message, "We are all liberals; we are all conservatives."

Russell Kirk has observed:

A great many people in both political parties, including most professors and most journalists, seem to be aware in some degree that American society is not secure from the menace of political totalitarianism. . . . Almost no one in the United States desires the coming of the total state: conservatives, and liberals old style, and liberals new style, and even most radicals, are unanimous in denouncing such a new order.[2]

The concern of the liberals stems from an early commitment to the individualism of John Locke. The commitment made it expedient in emergency to turn to the national government for the protection of individual liberty, a kind of pragmatic call for the assertion of national power to solve all the country's ills. The disquiet among liberals today flows from a new concern over their success—a reflection about the participation of the citizen in his government, about the precedence of efficient accomplishment of programs over other greater human and individual values.

The conservative arrives at his concern through a route more easily traced. The American Revolution was based on the need for checks and balances—a written constitution, protection of the minority against the majority, a belief in the division of powers, belief in a government of laws, and establishment of a judiciary.

The states will need the best features of conservatism and liberalism if the federal system is to be reformed and improved, and if the states are to be more effective within that system. We will need the hesitancy of the conservative in making sure that the nation does not cut itself off from its past and from the support of the people; we will need the dynamic optimism and the humanity of the liberal who insists government must change and expand and adapt itself to new conditions of thought and events.

It is testimony to the inner forces of the American people that they can change with the advancing tide of history.

They have seen the position of the original states change, but their wisdom has caused them to pause before abandoning an essential institution. I have confidence that a people whose every article of faith is a testament of freedom will shape a strong role for the states in harmony with the American destiny. The oversights and neglects, the discrimination and the poverty, the gap between the good life and the meager existence, are arousing the American people and forging within them the commitment to do more. The American people, who for so long restrained the full use of the resources of state governments in dealing with the ever-pressing problems of the nation, have now begun to be more receptive to the imperatives for reform.

The great American contribution to mankind has been the union of government and freedom. The states historically furnished their share of the initiatives and political strengths making this achievement possible, and they must continue to do so.

A new era of state reform is inevitable; that this will lead to a reordering of state institutions is natural; and that this will inaugurate a new spirit of state leadership bodes well for all that America has ever meant for all the peoples on earth.

In the final analysis, survival of the federal system rests with the people. For they are the supreme law in a democracy. Their will breathes life into the documents and the laws, and their combined agreement to be governed pumps vitality into the structure. For the revitalization of the states, all America can be united.

1. Testimony of Henry Steele Commager, before U.S. Congress, Senate, Committee on Foreign Relations, *Hearings, Changing American Attitudes toward Foreign Policy*, 90th. Cong., 1st. Sess., February 20, 1967.
2. Russell Kirk, *A Program for Conservatives*, (Chicago: Henry Regnery Company, 1954), p. 259.

INDEX

ACIR, 85, 141, 153, 163, 169
Adams, John, 207
Advisory Commission on Intergovernmental Relations, 85, 141, 153, 163, 169
Agnew, Spiro T., 146
Agriculture, 70–73, 126
Agricultural Adjustment Act, 70
Agriculture Extension Service, 72, 126
Alabama, 29, 205n7.
Alaska, 158n12., 206n12.
Allen, Ethan, 111
American Commonwealth, The, 39
Anaconda Copper, 33
Anderson, John, 182
Anderson, William, 103
Appalachia, 115
Arizona, 33, 205n6.
Arizona Employment Security Commission, 126
Arkansas, 205n6.
Articles of Confederation, 8, 17–18, 31
Association of Chief State School Officers, 116
Atlanta, Ga., 138
Atomic Energy Commission, 162
Automobile industry, 86–87
Automobile Manufacturers Association, 87
Avery, William H., 145

Babcock Foundation, 174
Bagdikian, Ben, 48–49
Bance, Frank, 114
Beard, Charles and Mary, 18
Berne, Eric, 87
Bill of Rights, 17, 19
Biossat, Bruce, 47
Blue Earth County, Minn., 124–125
Bowers, Edison, 76
Brandeis, Louis D., 55

Breathitt, Edward T., 58–59
Brinkley, David, 37
Broder, David, 191
Brown, Edmund G., 57–58
Bryce, James, 39
Buckley, William F., Jr., 177
Burke, Edmund, 207
Burns, James MacGregor, 2

California, 33, 58–59, 111, 176
  constitution, 29, 139
  taxes, 27, 146, 148
Campbell, Jack M., 120
Capital punishment, 4
Cardoza, Benjamin, 29
Carnegie Corporation, 117, 120
Casa Grande, Arizona, 125–127
Catalog of Federal Aids to State and Local Governments, 89
Chafee, John H., 112, 117
Chicago, Ill., 134
Christian Science Monitor, 86
Cimarron (movie), 84
Cities, 24, 25, 79, 102, 123–143, 162
Citizens Conference on State Legislatures, 182
Civil Defense Administration, 125
Civil War, 19–20
Coastal Plains, 115
Collins, Leroy, 35–36
Colorado River, 113
Combs, Bert T., 58
Committee for Economic Development, 148, 164
Compact for Education, 116–119
"Comprehensive Health Planning and Public Health Services Amendments, The," 155, 170
Conant, James B., 116, 118
Congress, 2, 35
  grants, 84–91, 99–101, 159, 170
  role, 19, 168, 171–72, 178
Connecticut, 21n3., 33, 140, 158n13.

213